OSCAR WILDE
A LIFE IN QUOTES

OSCAR WILDE

A LIFE IN QUOTES

EDITED AND
ANNOTATED BY
BARRY DAY

metro

First published in Great Britain in 2000
by Metro Books (an imprint of Metro Publishing Limited),
19 Gerrard Street, London W1V 7LA

British Library Cataloguing in Publication Data.
A CIP record of this book is available on request from
the British Library.

ISBN 1 84241 003 2
10 9 8 7 6 5 4 3 2 1

Designed and typeset by Ken Wilson
Printed in Great Britain by CPD Group, Wales

Frontispiece: 'Oscar', drawing by Lynne Carey

CONTENTS

LIST OF ILLUSTRATIONS

All illustrations are from the collection of Merlin Holland unless otherwise indicated.

LIST OF ILLUSTRATIONS

LIST OF ILLUSTRATIONS

FOR LYNNE...

...as ever

INTRODUCTION

Lithograph of Oscar from a drawing by
Thomas Maitland Cleland, 1882

I was a man who stood in symbolic relationship to the art and culture of my age. I had
realised this for myself at the very dawn of
my manhood, and had forced my age to
realise it afterwards.

(*De Profundis*)

For he who lives more lives than one
More deaths than one must die.

('The Ballad of Reading Gaol')

I'll be a poet, a writer, a dramatist, somehow
or other I'll be famous, or if not famous I'll
be notorious.

(In conversation at Oxford)

OSCAR WILDE'S LIFE was a play. To begin with it seemed a high comedy – at times even a farce – but as the years went by it took on the aspect of a Greek tragedy. Wilde himself seemed torn between being its hero and its critic. When the Eumenides (in the form of the London police) reluctantly arrived to arrest him – having given him every opportunity to flee the country – he seemed determined to stay and see how the plot turned out. ('One cannot keep going abroad unless one is a missionary, or what comes to the same thing, a commercial traveller.')

By doing so, he invalidated one of his own key precepts that 'to become a spectator of one's own life is to escape the suffering of life'. He could not believe that this was really happening to Oscar Wilde. His list of options had just reduced itself to one – henceforth he would be notorious, a media celebrity almost a century before they were to be invented.

In retrospect, it was probably inevitable. Few societies like being criticised for their superficiality and hypocrisy – particularly one as firmly entrenched in its moral rectitude and apparently effortless superiority as late Victorian England. The fact that its more perceptive members could see the hairline cracks of disintegration made them even more sensitive, particularly to the comments of someone they had allowed into their midst and reluctantly accepted as 'one of us'. The fellow, after all, was an *Irishman*, dammit!

Had Wilde simply criticised but otherwise personally conformed, he might possibly have got away with it but, instead, he positively articulated quite another view of life. He believed – or claimed to believe – that manners mattered more than morals and that beauty was its own religion:

To discern the beauty of a thing is the finest

point to which we can arrive. Even a colour-sense is more important, in the development of the individual, than a sense of right and wrong... There is in us a beauty-sense, separate from the other senses and above them, separate from the reason and of nobler import, separate from the soul and of equal value...

('The Critic As Artist')

Hedonism was the creed he preached, a loosely coherent set of values, drawn in the main from his understanding and interpretation of the ancient Greeks and the freedom of their way of life. As early as the age of sixteen 'the wonder and beauty of the old Greek life began to dawn on me... I began to read Greek eagerly. And the more I read the more I was enthralled.' He would later claim that, 'Whatever, in fact, is modern in our life we owe to the Greeks. Whatever is an anachronism is due to medievalism.'

Coupled with an extravagance of personal dress and a marked affectation of manner, this 'pagan' view of life was not calculated to endear him to his peers. What it did do, however, was to achieve the instant notoriety he sought. Attending a London theatre with a friend, he overheard the remark, 'There goes that bloody fool, Oscar Wilde.' Languidly he turned to the friend: 'It's extraordinary how soon one gets known in London.' For the man who liked to offer the advice, 'If you wish for reputation and fame in the world and success during your lifetime, you are right to take every opportunity of advertising yourself', it was proof positive, indeed, that it pays to advertise.

The unwitting tragedy in the making was that Wilde's complex nature prevented him from seeing clearly what he was achieving *besides* visibility. He was perfectly able to include himself in his criticisms of society and its institutions.

The pose was all part of the game of irony – a game at which he happened to be particularly gifted. Surely everyone could see that? But many of them never chose to. They merely awaited their time.

By the standards of many of his contemporaries, Wilde's literary output was not large: a number of poems, which he personally rated highly but which now appear, by and large, student exercises in fond imitation of the Latin and Greek masters ('more rhyme than reason'); a handful of controversial essays; all too few charming fairy stories ('It is the duty of every father to write fairy tales for his children'); and, of course, the plays, most particularly the great sequence of four that was cut short by the Queensberry affair.

The man that emerges from the words is variously clever and complex: often contemptuous yet caring; censorious yet sensitive; arrogant yet naïve; affected yet playful; ironic yet innocent; intuitive yet unaware. It was a fascinating yet fatal combination of qualities for its context and its time.

By the time of *De Profundis*, the long and rambling autobiographical letter he wrote in Reading prison, he was objective enough to see that he had 'let myself be lured into long spells of senseless and sensual ease. I amused myself by becoming a *flâneur,* a dandy, a man of fashion... I became the spendthrift of my own genius.'

Genius was a word Wilde coveted and used frequently in relation to himself – not always ironically. On first meeting French writer André Gide, he told him:

Voulez-vous savoir le grand drame de ma vie? C'est que j'ai mis mon génie dans ma vie; je n'ai mis que mon talent dans mes oeuvres.

(Do you want to know the great tragedy of my life? I've put all of my genius into my life; all I've put into my work is my talent.)

As with a lot of his aphorisms and epigrams, the neatly balanced form of words caught the moment but did not survive too close an inspection. In many ways his life *was* his work – and his life was talk.

Like the cynical Sir Henry Wotton in *The Picture of Dorian Gray* – a character Wilde later admitted he had based partly on himself as conversationalist:

He played with the idea, grew wilful; tossed it into the air and transformed it; let it escape and recaptured it; made it iridescent with fancy, and winged with paradox... It was an extraordinary improvisation.

The cynicism, incidentally, was a perfect camouflage for serious observation but Wilde feared it might sound less than sophisticated and even – heaven help us – sincere.

'I was the best talker ever seen at Oxford,' he would remember proudly, forgetting for the moment to turn the unvarnished thought into an axiom. For once, others placed his achievements even higher. George Bernard Shaw rated him as 'incomparably the greatest talker of his time – perhaps of *all* time.'

Robert Louis Stevenson once expressed the view that, 'The first duty for man is to speak: that is his chief business in the world.' And how Wilde spoke – on anything and everything, on matters he knew well and they were many (the surface dressing of the dandy tended to disguise a mind that had won him an Oxford double first in classics and philosophy). And when he was out of his depth, he would simply invent – but always with the carefully chosen words in the perfectly formed sentences, spoken in a low, musical voice 'like velvet' that would invariably charm its particular audience, so that even those who came to sneer at the man would stay to enjoy and applaud his wit. Even the fact that his conversation was closer to monologue and that 'he listened like one accustomed to speak' never served to detract from the effect he created.

There was an ironic ambivalence in society's attitude towards him in the early years of his success. Men tended to dislike him, sight unseen, since what they had heard convinced them he was not, in their terms, 'manly'. Their suspicions were then confirmed when their womenfolk invariably found Wilde attractive. He seemed to understand women instinctively and to be genuinely interested in their stirrings towards self-expression and independence. Unlike their husbands or admirers, he was actually prepared to *listen*. As the Duchess in *Dorian Gray* observes: 'We women love with our ears, just as you men love with your eyes, if you ever love at all.' Perhaps part of the secret was that *what* they heard was an underlying sympathy for life. The Wilde wit would caress more often than cut. And always it would explore.

There were those who would find it frustrating to try and pin down his position on an issue. Surely he'd said quite the opposite only the other day? But then, who said he had to agree with himself all the time? It became something of a game to lead the listener or reader along a certain path and then reverse direction. 'Not that I agree with everything I have said in this essay,' he wrote in 'The Critic As Artist', '[it] simply represents an artistic standpoint, and in aesthetic criticism, attitude is everything.' Many of the things he said were said simply to provoke. As Basil Hallward says to Lord Henry in *Dorian Gray*: 'I don't believe that . . . and I don't believe you do either.'

In a later generation, another playful verbal philosopher, Marshall McLuhan, would suffer from the same kind of heavy-handed criticism for setting up a point of view, publicly examining, then abandoning it. The techniques of academia were not, it appeared, readily transferable to the society *salon*. Yet Wilde was inherently a teacher and the habit died hard.

Were the witticisms all carefully honed in the silence of the study and then packaged, ready to be inserted into the next day's discourse, rather like the stand-up comedian does today? To begin with, perhaps. When his sometime friend, journalist Frank Harris, first met Wilde in 1884, he found that his conversation consisted 'chiefly of epigrams almost mechanically constructed of proverbs and familiar sayings turned upside down . . . much of it mere topsy-turvy paradox'. Like many great comedians, it would be surprising if he had not laid down a store of 'lines' which he could recall when the occasion demanded. Yeats was inclined to believe that many of Wilde's remarks were crafted 'overnight with labour and yet all spontaneous'. Even some of the exchanges in court – which *were* spontaneous – have all the elements of a 'crosstalk' act:

> WILDE: Iced champagne is a favourite drink of mine – strongly against my doctor's orders.
>
> EDWARD CARSON, QC: Never mind your doctor's orders, sir!
>
> WILDE: I never do.

Certainly, he did something similar with the printed word. Many of the best lines in the late plays had their origins, for instance, in *Dorian Gray* (1891). None the less, when they made the transition, a change of word or emphasis would invariably show Wilde the careful craftsman at work, polishing what had appeared earlier in a less perfected form.

The plays undoubtedly convey the essential flavour of his talk – almost all the parts can be seen to be Wilde himself in one disguise or another – and the form of dramatic discourse he was perfecting when his personal curtain fell was promising to be the ideal public medium for his unique talents. Humour was the means of attracting his audience's attention and allowing him to mask his criticisms of its behaviour. The theatre was the drawing room that seated hundreds every night who also paid for the privilege of hearing him talk.

The point that is often missed about Wilde is that he was not merely a man who produced witty remarks on a production line. He was a man who was possessed of a genuinely humorous *attitude* to life – and he included himself in that cosmic view: 'The comic spirit is a necessity in life as a purge to all human vanity.' The fact that his audience did not appreciate that greater joke was their tragedy and, ultimately, his.

His style was not without its critics. Herbert Asquith (later to become Prime Minister) once accused him of overdoing the use of italics for emphasis, like the man who talks louder in order to make himself heard, to which Wilde replied:

The brilliant phrase, like good wine, needs no bush. But just as the orator marks his good things by a dramatic pause, or by raising or lowering his voice, or by gesture, so the writer marks his epigrams with italics, setting the little gem, so to speak, like a jeweller.

The printed word is enshrined but Wilde left all too little.

The conversation dies with the memory of those who were there to hear it. And there the debate over the spontaneity of Wilde's wit might remain – except for the transcripts of his three court cases, where his replies were clearly unrehearsed, since few of the questions could have been anticipated.

Here was Wilde at his best and worst... effortlessly deflecting a crude question with an elegantly ironic answer that would draw laughter or even appreciative applause from the spectators... then succumbing to the fatal intellectual arrogance that would lure him into an epigram too far. When asked whether a piece of prose was not immoral, he could not refrain from answering, 'It was worse; it was badly written.' And when asked if he had 'ever adored a young man madly', he answered, 'I have never given adoration to anybody except myself.'

For those few days he played to a new audience of the general public and found that, although they, too, appreciated his turn of phrase, the ironic frivolity of his view of life was over *their* heads, too. He was, it appeared, irrevocably out of joint with his time. It was time for his play to end.

And end it did with the pity and terror appropriate to Greek tragedy. His prison sentence produced two final works: his personal apologia, *De Profundis*, and the epic poem, 'The Ballad of Reading Gaol'. And then – nothing. After his release there were three pathetic years of impoverished exile but the will to write had left him.

Just before the end in 1900 he told a friend in Paris, 'I wrote when I did not know life. Now that I do know the meaning of life, I have no more to write.' He died unsure whether his reputation, his 'genius' – the one thing that really mattered to him – would survive his disgrace. Had his life truly been, as he once said, 'all conversation and no action'?

In the event, his concern was groundless. One hundred

years after his death, when it comes to the epigrammatic quotation, only Dr Johnson, Noël Coward and Mark Twain come even close. And perhaps the greatest tribute – and one which he would have appreciated – is that when we are unsure of the origin of a line we like, we invariably attribute it to Oscar Wilde.

At an exhibition of his friend Whistler's paintings, a gauche art critic called one of them bad. In Wilde's hearing the artist sharply corrected the critic:

> My dear fellow, you must never say that a painting's good or bad. Good or bad are not terms to be used by you. Say 'I like this' and 'I dislike that' and you'll be within your right. And now come and have a whiskey. You're sure to like that.

'I wish *I* had said that,' Wilde exclaimed. To which the perceptive Whistler replied, 'You *will*, Oscar, you will!'

NOTE:

The words of Wilde are derived from the published work, the more than one thousand letters that have survived and from the many biographies and reminiscences. An insurmountable problem when dealing with someone whose *chef d'oeuvre* was the fleeting art of conversation is to know whether the recollection in tranquillity was ever completely accurate but I have done what I can to cross-check references.

What emerges dramatically by attempting to tell Wilde's own story in his own words is that he was incidentally telling it all the time, irrespective of the apparent content of what he wrote. No matter into whose mouth he put the specific words, aspects of Oscar insist on emerging. In many ways he was his only subject.

In *A Life in Quotes* you will, of course, find the public Wilde polishing the verbal jewels that bought him fame but you will also hear the private Wilde struggling with words to make sense of a less than perfect world. The man who emerges is no less impressive as a literary figure but much more likeable as a human being than one had perhaps expected.

BARRY DAY

2000

PART ONE

THE 'PROFESSIONAL IRISHMAN'

OSSIAN (WITH VARIATIONS).
THE SON OF IA-CULTCHA.

IS THIS THE SON OF CULTCHA'S SHADOWY FORM?

Punch *cartoon, 1882*

If one could only teach the English how to talk, and the Irish how to listen, society here would be quite civilised.

(Mrs Cheveley in *An Ideal Husband*)

OSCAR FINGAL O'FLAHERTIE WILLS WILDE was born in Dublin on 16 October 1854, the second son of Sir William and Lady Jane Wilde. His mother was a rabid Irish Nationalist and wrote fiery verse and prose under the pen name of 'Speranza' (meaning 'Hope'). She was to be a key literary influence on him and in *De Profundis* he was to claim – somewhat wistfully – that she should rank 'intellectually' with Elizabeth Barrett Browning and 'historically' with Madame Roland. Lady Wilde would probably have concurred.

Wilde was proud of his heritage. He considered the Irish race 'the most aristocratic in Europe' and insisted to Frank Harris that:

> The O'Flaherties were kings in Ireland and I have a right to the name. I am descended from them.

Lady Speranza Wilde, 1864

Early in life, however, he realised that in terms of 'marquee value' a name of such complexity might prove a hindrance:

> My name has two 'O's, two 'F's, and two 'W's. A name which is destined to be in everybody's mouth must not be too long. It comes so expensive in advertisements. When one is unknown, a number of Christian names are useful, perhaps needful. As one becomes famous, one sheds some of them, just as a balloonist… rising higher, sheds unnecessary ballast. All but two (Oscar Fingal) of my five names have been thrown overboard. Soon I shall discard another and be known simply as 'The Wilde' or 'The Oscar'.

Some of his fellow students were clearly not privy to the master plan and – in recognition of his comportment, which was even then eccentric for its time – caricatured him as 'O'Flighty'.

His mother and father were both Hibernophiles and throughout his life – long after he had settled in England and carefully erased the Irish accent – Wilde would proclaim the virtues of his native land. He told Harris:

> The Irish were civilised and Christians when the English kept themselves warm with tattooings.

The English in his view had much to answer for:

> With the coming of the English, art in

Ireland came to an end, and it has had no
existence for over seven hundred years.

On his American tour in 1882 he was interviewed by the
Philadelphia Press. Lord Cavendish, Chief Secretary for
Ireland, had recently been assassinated in Phoenix Park
and Wilde was asked for his views:

When liberty comes with hands dabbled in
blood, it is hard to shake hands with her. We
forget how much England is to blame. She is
reaping the fruit of seven centuries of
injustice.

Later he was to be more epigrammatic about Irish home
rule, an event that would not take place until 1921...

My own idea is that Ireland should rule
England.

(In conversation)

... even though he was without illusions about his own
countrymen. In 1888 he confided to Irish poet, W. B.
Yeats...

We Irish are too poetical to be poets. We are
a nation of brilliant failures but we are the
greatest talkers since the Greeks.

... and to poet, Ernest Dowson...

I keep on building castles of fairy gold in the
air: we Celts always do.

(1897)

[5]

His two most distinguished contemporaries always had Wilde's measure. Yeats was 'astonished by this scholar who as a man of the world was so perfect', while Shaw was, typically, more beady in his assessment: 'A very Irish Irishman, and as such, a foreigner everywhere but in Ireland.' Then he, too – like Sheridan, Goldsmith and so many professional Irishmen, before and since – took himself off across the water to tell the English what they were doing wrong.

PART TWO

EDUCATION

The young Wilde at Oxford, 1878

Education is an admirable thing, but it is well to remember from time to time that nothing that is worth knowing can be taught.

('The Critic As Artist')

Ignorance is like a delicate exotic fruit; touch it and the bloom is gone.

(Lady Bracknell in *The Importance of Being Earnest*)

To expect the unexpected shows a thoroughly modern intellect.

(Mrs Cheveley in *An Ideal Husband*)

I have forgotten all about my schooldays. I have a vague impression that they were detestable.

(Mrs Cheveley in *An Ideal Husband*)

WILDE ATTENDED the Portora Royal School, Enniskillen from 1864 until he won a scholarship to Trinity College, Dublin in 1871. The experience left several permanent impressions. He did not like sport, particularly football:

> I never liked to kick or be kicked. Football is all very well as a game for rough girls, but it is hardly suitable for delicate boys.
>
> (In conversation)

Not that rowing was much better:

> This is indeed a form of death, and entirely incompatible with any belief in the immortality of the soul.

In fact:

> The only possible exercise is talk. It is so exhausting not to talk.
>
> (In an interview)

And he formed a lifelong aversion to the teaching profession:

> How appalling is that ignorance which is the inevitable result of the fatal habit of imparting opinions!
>
> ('The Critic As Artist')

> We teach people how to remember, we never teach them how to grow.
>
> ('The Critic As Artist')

Dr Chasuble is a most learned man. He has never written a single book, so you can imagine how much he knows.

(Cecily in *The Importance of Being Earnest*)

Everybody who is incapable of learning has taken to teaching – that is really what our enthusiasm for education has come to.

('The Decay of Lying')

Nor was he particularly impressed by learning:

Learned conversation is either the affectation of the ignorant or the profession of the mentally unemployed.

('The Critic As Artist')

Intellect is in itself a mode of exaggeration, and destroys the harmony of any face. The moment one sits down to think, one becomes all nose, or all forehead, or something.

(Lord Henry Wotton in *The Picture of Dorian Gray*)

To have been well brought up is a great drawback nowadays. It shuts one out from so much.

(Lady Hunstanton in *A Woman of No Importance*)

In 1874, Wilde was awarded a demyship to Magdalen College, Oxford. Ireland was gone but by no means forgotten, although:

> My Irish accent was one of the many things I forgot at Oxford.

At the end of his life he would recall:

> The two turning points in my life were when my father sent me to Oxford and when Society sent me to prison.

And he would tell Frank Harris:

> Oxford – the mere word to me is full of an inexpressible and incommunicable charm... the home of lost causes and impossible ideals ...Oxford is the capital of romance... in its own way as memorable as Athens.

In a letter to a student *protégé* not long before Wilde died, the memory was still green:

> Oxford... the most flower-like time of one's life. One sees the shadows of things in silver mirrors. Later on one sees the gorgon's head, and one suffers, because it does not turn one to stone.
>
> (Letter to Louis Wilkinson)

I remember bright young faces, and grey

misty quadrangles, Greek forms passing
through Gothic cloisters, life playing among
ruins and, what I loved best in the world,
Poetry and Paradox dancing together.
(Letter to Harry Marillier, 1885)

It was 'the most beautiful thing in England' but (he would
report prophetically):

God! How I wasted my life up here! I look
back on weeks and months of extravagance,
trivial talk, utter vacancy of employment
with feelings so bitter that I have lost faith in
myself – I am too ridiculously easily led
astray. I do nothing but write sonnets and
scribble poetry.
(Letter to William Ward, 1877)

Perhaps, after all, Oxford's dreaming spires encouraged a
little too much dreaming?

If you had been sent to Cambridge to study
science, instead of to Oxford to dawdle over
literature, you would know that a hypoth-
esis that explains everything is a certainty.
(*The Portrait of Mr W. H.*)

But Wilde was an Oxford man through and through. To be
one was to embody all the qualities worth having:

Untruthful! My nephew Algernon?
Impossible! He is an Oxonian.
(Lady Bracknell in *The Importance of Being Earnest*)

My boy is excessively immoral... And he's
only left Oxford a few months – I really
don't know what they teach them there.
(Duchess of Berwick in *Lady Windermere's Fan*)

✐

At times, being morbid... [he wrote to
Jerome Pollitt in 1898]... I am bored by the
lack of intellect: but this is a grave fault. I
attribute it to Oxford. None of us survive
culture.

And when, in prison, he came to weigh up the many failings
of his lover, Bosie (Lord Alfred Douglas), just about the
most damning criticism he could call to mind was that the
infidel had 'been at my own College at Oxford'.

Whatever people may say against
Cambridge, it is certainly the best
preparatory school for Oxford that I know.
(Letter to Robert Ross, *c.*1888)

One small piece of prophecy when he was in residence himself was his remark on observing an Oxford athlete in
training:

His left leg is a Greek poem.

(He was to say the same thing about Henry Irving – without specifying that the poem was Greek!)

At Trinity he had begun to cultivate his taste for the
manners, *mores* and aesthetics of ancient Greece. Upon
that basis he began to construct his own personal credo and

define what, in *The Picture of Dorian Gray*, he would consider an ideal type of Oxford youth:

> That was to combine something of the real
> culture of the scholar with all the grace and
> distinction and perfect manner of a citizen of
> the world. Young Oxonians are very
> delightful, so Greek and graceful and
> uneducated.

(Letter to Violet Fane, 1886)

THE SIX-MARK TEA-POT.

Æsthetic Bridegroom. "IT IS QUITE CONSUMMATE, IS IT NOT?"
Intense Bride. "IT IS, INDEED! OH, ALGERNON, LET US LIVE UP TO IT!"

Punch's *comment on Oscar's preoccupation
with blue china, 1888*

[*14*]

Part of the 'perfect manner' was to surround oneself with beautiful objects. It was at this time that he determined that the lily and the sunflower – both of which became Wilde trademarks – were the perfect flowers.

> These two lovely flowers are in England the most perfect models of design, the most naturally adapted for the decorative art.

He also joined the fashionable cult of blue china and acquired a pair of Sèvres vases. His observation that, 'I find it harder every day to live up to my blue china' produced a predictable reaction from his more orthodox and hearty contemporaries.

So taken was he with all matters Hellenic that he embarked on a long trip to Greece with his old classics tutor from Trinity. When he returned late, he was immediately rusticated for the rest of the term. He boasted that he was 'sent down from Oxford for being the first undergraduate to visit Olympia'.

Two men exerted important influences over him during those Oxford years and in many ways they were the making of the mature Wilde. John Ruskin (1819–1900) was then the Slade Professor of Art. It was he who sparked Wilde's interest in intellectual matters and caused him to question the nature of his faith. He saw Ruskin as:

> Something of prophet, of priest and of poet, and to you the gods gave eloquence such as they have given to none other, so that your message might come to us with the fire of passion and the marvel of music, making the deaf to hear and the blind to see.

Ruskin was 'a sort of exquisite romantic flower; like a violet filling the whole air with the ineffable perfume of belief', although later Wilde was to say, 'It was his poetry I loved, not his piety.' 'The dearest memories of my Oxford days,' he wrote to Ruskin in 1888, 'are my walks and talks with you, and from you I learned nothing but what was good.'

He learned a very different and more decadent doctrine from Walter Pater (1839–94). Pater was a Fellow of Brasenose College and, if Ruskin represented faith, Pater espoused a dangerously heady mysticism. Conventions were for the conventional. One should live one's life for beauty and pleasure. In Wilde he found a ready-made acolyte.

> [Pater] taught me the highest form of art: the austerity of beauty... I learned the instrument of speech with him, for I could see by his face when I had said something extraordinary.

These strong contrary forces buffeted Wilde throughout his Oxford career. Born a Protestant, he was powerfully attracted to the 'Scarlet Woman' of Roman Catholicism but was unable to commit. Instead, he temporarily gave way to the ritual appeal of Masonry, though it seems clear that the gorgeous pomp and properties had just as much appeal as the masonic mysteries! None of which helped his studies:

> The whole theory of modern education is radically unsound. Fortunately, in England, at any rate, education produces no effect whatsoever. If it did, it would prove a serious danger to the upper classes, and probably lead to acts of violence in Grosvenor Square.
>
> (Lady Bracknell in *The Importance of Being Earnest*)

Examinations are of no value whatsoever.
If a man is a gentleman, he knows quite
enough, and if he is not a gentleman,
whatever he knows is bad for him.

(Lord Illingworth in *A Woman of No Importance*)

In examinations the foolish ask questions
the wise cannot answer.

('Phrases and Philosophies for the Use of the Young')

To know nothing of their great men is one of
the necessary elements of English education.

Despite the distractions, Wilde achieved a 'double first' in
Greats – classical literature and philosophy. During his *viva
voce* examination he was asked to translate a passage from
the Greek version of the New Testament. Having done so to
the satisfaction of the examiners, he was stopped. 'Oh, do
let me go on,' he was supposed to have said, 'I want to see
how it ends.'

Surprisingly, in view of his disaffection for the teaching
profession, he was to seriously consider joining it. As late as
1885, he is writing to his contemporary, George (later Lord)
Curzon, asking for a position as Inspector of Schools. It was
possibly the only time he was tempted to tread a conventional path.

When his friend William Ward asked him about his
plans after Oxford, Wilde replied:

God knows. I won't be a dried-up Oxford
don, anyhow.

In an 1877 letter to another friend, Reginald Harding, he was more introspective:

> This is an era in my life, a crisis – I wish I could look into the seeds of Time and see what is coming.

Years later in *De Profundis*:

> I remember when I was at Oxford saying to one of my friends ... that I wanted to taste the fruit of all the trees in the garden of the world with that passion in my soul. And so, indeed, I went out, and so lived.

When he left, he styled himself a 'Professor of Aesthetics and a Critic of Art'. His task was now to prove it.

PART THREE

YOUTH

*Wilde as a fashionable
undergraduate, 1876*

Youth is the Lord of Life. Youth has a king-
dom waiting for it.

(Lord Illingworth in *A Woman of No Importance*)

Those whom the gods love grow young.

('A Few Maxims for the Instruction of the Over-Educated')

Youth! Youth! There is absolutely nothing in
the world but Youth!

(Lord Henry Wotton in *The Picture of Dorian Gray*)

YOUTH WAS a lifelong obsession for Wilde. Unfortunately for him, he appreciated its advantages more in retrospect and most of his aphorisms deal with its loss – sometimes quite bitterly:

> Only youth has a right to crown an artist.
> That is the real privilege of youth, if youth
> only knew it.
>
> (*De Profundis*)

> Youth isn't an affectation. Youth is an art.
>
> (Lord Goring in *An Ideal Husband*)

> The condition of perfection is idleness: the
> aim of perfection is youth.
>
> ('Phrases and Philosophies for the Use of the Young')

In *The Picture of Dorian Gray*, he encapsulated the some-times contradictory views that were to bedevil his later years and which were to be brought up time and again in his court cases:

> There is nothing like youth. The middle-
> aged are mortgaged to life. The old are in
> life's lumber-room. But Youth is the Lord of
> life. Youth has a kingdom waiting for it.
>
> (Lord Illingworth in *A Woman of No Importance*)

The old believe everything: the middle-aged suspect everything: the young know everything.

('Phrases and Philosophies for the Use of the Young')

The tragedy of old age is not that one is old, but that one is young.

Dorian Gray was Wilde's idealisation of youth, someone he admitted he would like to have been 'in another age', a man so dedicated to the idea of eternal youth that he bargained his life away in pursuit of it – only to find that he had pursued a chimera:

What a pity that in life we only get our lessons when they are of no use to us.

(Lady Windermere in *Lady Windermere's Fan*)

LORD ILLINGWORTH: I never intend to grow old. The soul is born old but grows young. That is the comedy of life.
MRS ALLONBY: And the body is born young and grows old. That is life's tragedy.

(*A Woman of No Importance*)

In Wilde's view – as expressed by his characters – there was little benefit in maturity...

As soon as people are old enough to know better, they don't know anything at all.

(Mr Graham in *Lady Windermere's Fan*)

Short of aping Dorian Gray, the passing of the years had to be reluctantly accepted. Otherwise, the price was really unduly exorbitant. Dorian's irreverent mentor, Lord Henry Wotton, was adamant on the subject:

To get back my youth I would do anything in the world, except take exercise, get up early, or be respectable.

Youth! There's nothing like it. It's absurd to talk of the ignorance of youth. The only people to whose opinion I listen now with any respect are people much younger than myself.

That inordinate passion for pleasure which is the secret of remaining young.
(Lady Windermere in 'Lord Arthur Savile's Crime')

Your views are terribly unsound. I am afraid that you have been listening to the views of someone older than yourself.
('The Critic As Artist')

I have never learned anything except from people younger than myself.
(Letter to Cambridge student Harry Marillier, 1886)

Although he did have one possible scenario to suggest:

> To get back one's youth, one merely has to repeat one's follies.

But perhaps, after all, Youth was yet another lost cause?

> What was youth at best? A green, an unripe time, a time of shallow moods and sickly thoughts.
>
> (*The Picture of Dorian Gray*)

And as for *children*:

> Children begin by loving their parents. After a time they judge them. Rarely, if ever, do they forgive them.
>
> (Lord Illingworth in *A Woman of No Importance*)

(This is an interesting example of Wilde 'polishing' a line. When he used it in *Dorian Gray*, he was prepared to admit that 'sometimes they forgive them'.)

> The youth of the present day are quite monstrous. They have absolutely no respect for dyed hair.
>
> (Mr Dumby in *Lady Windermere's Fan*)

With the inevitable result:

> Few parents nowadays pay any regard to what their children say to them. The old-fashioned respect for the young is fast dying out.
>
> (Gwendolen in *The Importance of Being Earnest*)

Not that matters were any better in America:

> From its earliest years every American child
> spends most of its time correcting the faults
> of its father and mother... In America the
> young are always ready to give to those who
> are older than themselves the full benefits of
> their inexperience.

The breakdown of family values finally produced one of
Wilde's best-known lines:

> To lose one parent may be regarded as a
> misfortune... To lose both seems like
> carelessness.
>
> (Lady Bracknell in *The Importance of Being Earnest*)

None the less, youth – and the desire to stay young himself –
continued to haunt Wilde. The child in him was never far
from the surface. He told Frank Harris:

> I like people who are young, bright, happy,
> careless and original. I do not like them sens-
> ible, and I do not like them old; I don't like
> social distinctions of any kind, and the mere
> fact of youth is so wonderful that I would
> sooner talk to a young man for half an hour
> than be cross-examined by an elderly Q.C.

In this he was largely repeating in self-justification what he
had said in reply to the hostile questioning of Edward
Carson (the 'elderly Q.C.') at his first trial. Wilde and
Carson had been contemporaries at Trinity College,

Dublin. When he heard that Carson was to represent Queensberry, Wilde observed – 'No doubt he will perform his task with all the bitterness of an old friend.' And, indeed, he did. From the opening encounters, Carson probed his fellow student's weakest point. When asked his age, Wilde gave it as 39. Carson had every reason to know that he was, in fact, 41. It was a small enough point but it tinged Wilde's subsequent credibility.

The word 'old' is full of terror.
(Letter to Harry Marillier)

Around the time Wilde left Oxford, an American magazine was publishing a series of 'celebrity surveys'. He eagerly completed the one he received and it gives at least some idea of how he wished to be seen at that time:

Favourite Colour: *Couleur de rose*
Flower: *Lilium Amatum*
Tree: Stone pine and lemon tree
Object in Nature: The Sea (when there are no bathing machines)
Hour of the Day: Post Hour
Season of the Year: Beginning of Autumn
Perfume: Almond Blossoms
Gem: Sapphire in Winter. Diamond in Summer
Painters: Fra Angelico. Turner. Correggio
Poets: Euripides. Keats. Theocritus. And myself
Poetesses: Sappho and Lady Wilde

Prose Authors: Plato and John Ruskin

Characters in Romance: Achilles and Nausikaa

Characters in History: Dr Newman and Alexander

Books to take up for an hour: I never take up books for an hour

What book would you part with last?: My Euripides

What epoch would you have chosen to have lived in?: The Italian Renaissance

Where would you like to live?: Florence and Rome

What is your favourite amusement?: Writing sonnets and riding

What trait of character do you most admire in a man?: The power of attracting friends

What trait of character do you most admire in a woman?: The power of becoming either a Cleopatra or a St Catherine

What trait of character do you most detest?: Vanity, self-esteem, conceitedness

If not yourself, who would you rather be?: A Cardinal of the Catholic Church

What is your idea of happiness?: Absolute power over men's minds, even if accompanied by chronic toothache

What is your idea of misery?: Living a poor and respectable life in an obscure village

[27]

What is your *bête noire?*: A thorough Irish
Protestant

What is your dream?: Getting my hair cut

What do you believe to be your distinguishing
characteristics?: Inordinate self-esteem

What are the sublimest passions of which human
nature is capable?: Asceticism; ambition

What are the sweetest words in the world?: 'Well
done!'

What are the saddest words?: Failure

What is your aim in life?: Success, fame or even
notoriety

PART FOUR

AMERICA

'Something to "live up" to in America', 1882

I have nothing to declare but my genius.

(Wilde's supposed statement to US Customs officials on his arrival in the country)

Of course, if one had enough money to go to America, one would not go.

(In conversation)

We have really everything in common with America nowadays, except, of course, language.

('The Canterville Ghost')

'Perhaps, after all, America never has been discovered,' said Mr Erskine. 'I myself would say that it had merely been detected.'

(*The Picture of Dorian Gray*)

Of course, America had often been discovered before Columbus, but it had always been hushed up.

(Attributed)

AFTER THE SUCCESS of Oxford, the 'Professor of Aesthetics' found himself at something of a loose end. He wrote his first play – *Vera, or the Nihilists* (1880) – but could find no one to produce it. He published his own collected and somewhat derivative *Poems* – at his own expense – but the fame he was so desperately seeking for the moment eluded him. Even he had to admit that his verse was 'more rhyme than reason'.

Wilde began to cultivate what would become in the following century the art of celebrity – being famous for being well known and well known for being famous. Copies of his work would be dedicated to the really famous, accompanied by a note, carefully protecting the sender by stressing the author's youth. To Gladstone, for instance, he would write:

> I am little more than a boy, and have no literary interest in London, but perhaps if *you* saw any good stuff in the lines I send you, some editor… might publish them.

It soon became difficult to ignore his flamboyant figure around London with his long, flowing hair, velvet coat, knee breeches and black silk stockings. His unconventional views on all matters aesthetic – however little they were truly comprehended by his audience – also augmented the reputation, not to say the affectation.

When Gilbert and Sullivan were looking for a new subject for their successful series of Savoy operas, Wilde and the 'Aesthetic Movement' seemed ready-made. *Patience* opened in October 1881 at the Savoy and the character of Bunthorne, 'the fleshly poet' – though perhaps partly based on Rossetti – was generally considered to represent Wilde. When an American company was assembled by Richard

D'Oyly Carte, the Gilbert and Sullivan impresario, it was thought that Wilde's actual presence in the States would help the show's publicity. A lecture tour was rapidly put together and on 24 December 1881 he sailed for New York. He was to stay in America for over a year.

On Wilde's well-publicised arrival in America, he was greeted by reporters. He told them:

I am not exactly pleased with the Atlantic. It is not so majestic, or even as large, as I expected.

Lecturing in America, 1882

[*32*]

To the *New York World* reporter he confided:

> I came from England because I thought
> America was the best place to see.

With true American application, his hosts whisked him
from place to place. His various letters home give some idea
of his experience:

> I bow graciously and sometimes honour
> them with a royal observation. . . loving
> virtuous obscurity as I do, you can judge
> how much I dislike this lionizing. . .

> I have had a sort of triumphal progress, live
> like a young sybarite, travel like a young
> god. I am deluged with poems and flowers at
> every town.

> I wave a gloved hand and an ivory cane and
> they cheer… I give sittings to artists and
> generally behave as I have always behaved –
> *dreadfully*.

Over time the fictional element of the tour took on a life of
its own:

> I have several secretaries. One writes my
> autographs all day for my admirers [*he
> would later claim that this one had to go to
> the hospital with writer's cramp*] – the other

receives the flowers that are left really every ten minutes. A third whose hair resembles mine is obliged to send off locks of his own hair to the myriad maidens of the city, and so is rapidly becoming bald...

(Letter to Mrs George Lewis)

Wilde's appearance was every bit as important to the success of his lectures as what he said:

They were dreadfully disappointed at Cincinnati at my not wearing knee breeches.

Word of his apparel would precede him and relatively few of his audience would appreciate that his fanciful garb was, in fact, the costume of his Masonic lodge.

Strange that a pair of silk stockings should so upset a nation.

In America I have been face to face with people who have never seen good art... many come to hear me just from curiosity... The great thing is to get them to come.

But – in varying numbers – come they did, even if many of them came to laugh at, rather than with, this strange man who chose to talk about 'The House Beautiful' or 'The English Renaissance in Art' ('a sort of new birth of the spirit of man'). But then, as he said in one of his lectures:

Caricature is the tribute mediocrity pays to genius.

*Oscar Wilde on the American
lecture tour, 1882*

On 'Our English Renaissance' he had things like this to say:

> We want children to grow up in England in
> the simple atmosphere of all fair things, so
> that they will love what is beautiful and good
> and hate what is evil and ugly, long before
> they know the reason why.
>
> ('The House Beautiful')

He was busy collecting his own 'Personal Impressions' of this remarkable country:

> America is the noisiest country that ever
> existed. One is waked up in the morning not
> by the singing of the nightingale, but by the
> steam whistle.

> I only saw one reposeful American – a
> wooden figure outside a tobacco shop.

> In America life is one long expectoration.

> I only saw two processions: one was the Fire
> Brigade preceded by the Police, the other
> was the Police preceded by the Fire Brigade.

Rumour had it that showman P.T. Barnum offered him the equivalent of £200 if he would lead an elephant through the streets of New York carrying a lily in one hand and a sunflower in the other. Wilde apparently felt that was going too far even for him.

In going to America one learns that poverty is not a necessary accompaniment to Civilisation.

From one hotel window he saw a billboard advertising his talk and wrote to a friend:

I am now six feet high, printed, it is true, in those primary colours which I pass my life protesting, but even still it is fame and anything is better than virtuous obscurity, even one's name in alternate colours of Albert blue and magenta... I feel I have not lived in vain.

He felt free to criticise lack of beauty and taste when he encountered it – no matter what the cost ...

There is one article of furniture... that for absolutely horrid ugliness surpasses anything I have seen – the cast iron American stove...

... and when he was invited by the citizens of Griggsville, Kansas to lecture on aesthetics, he sent them a telegram:

BEGIN BY CHANGING THE NAME OF YOUR TOWN

However, there were many things that he found to admire:

A remarkable characteristic of the Americans

is the manner in which they have applied
science to modern life.

But, he added with ecological perception:

Why does science not clean the streets and
free the rivers from pollution?

By the vagaries of the tour's organisation, he found himself
randomly crisscrossing the country:

I don't know where I am: somewhere in the
middle of coyotes and *cãnons*: one is a 'ravine'
and the other a 'fox'. I don't know which,
but I think they change about.
(Letter to Mrs George Lewis)

The prairie reminded me of a piece of
blotting-paper.

The two most remarkable bits of scenery in
the States are undoubtedly Delmonico's
restaurant and the Yosemite Valley...
Delmonico's... has done more to promote a
good feeling between England and America
than anything else this century.
('Dinners and Dishes')

I have also lectured at Leadville, the greatest
mining city in the Rocky Mountains... My

audience was entirely miners; their make-up excellent, red shorts and blonde beards… [*He was to say that 'Colorado miners were the only well-dressed men I have seen in America'*] … I spoke to them of the early Florentines, and they slept as though no

BROTHER JONATHAN; AFTER VIEWING MR. OSCAR WILDE.

"WAL! ENGLAND HAS SENT US OUT MANY CURIOUS THINGS: BUT THIS WHIPS 'EM ALL. TAKE IT AWAY!"

America had never seen anything like Oscar, 1882

crime had ever stained the ravines of their
mountain home.

(Letter to Mrs Bernard Beere)

He then proceeded to read to the miners from Benvenuto
Cellini's autobiography:

I was reproved by my hearers for not having
brought him with me. I explained that he
had been dead for some little time, which
elicited the enquiry, 'Who shot him?'

One evening a member of the audience had brought along a
small baby. When Wilde asserted in his lecture that 'There
is no better way of loving Nature than through Art', the
baby burst into tears. 'I wish the juvenile enthusiast would
restrain its aesthetic raptures,' said Wilde, at which the
baby was immediately silent. On the same visit he was
taken down a mine in a bucket:

I, of course, true to my principle, being
graceful even in a bucket... when I lit a long
cigar and quaffed a couple of cocktails
without flinching, they cheered me till the
silver fell in glittering dust from the roof on
to our table and unanimously pronounced
me in their grand simple way 'a bully boy
with no glass eye'.

His reputation as a hard drinker now fully established, on
another occasion he was offered supper:

The first course being whiskey, the second

course being whiskey and the third course
also whiskey – but they still called it supper.

He was also taken to a saloon, where he was shown:

The only rational method of art criticism I
have ever come across. Over the saloon piano
was the notice: 'PLEASE DON'T SHOOT
THE PIANIST. HE IS DOING HIS BEST.'

He experienced good old American nostalgia for its glorious
– if all too recent – history. Remarking to an elderly
Southern gentleman on the beauty of the moon, he received
the reply – 'Yes, but you should have seen it before the
War!'

Not that he approved of everything that he saw. He
found Niagara Falls:

Simply a vast unnecessary amount of water
going the wrong way and then falling over
unnecessary rocks. . . Every American bride
is taken there and the sight of the
stupendous waterfall must be one of the
earliest, if not the keenest, disappointments
in American married life.

(In conversation)

In New York: 'the streets seemed paved with brass, and the
air made of lead'; 'one could dine in New York but not
dwell there'; Los Angeles was 'a sort of Naples'; Boston 'an
invention'; San Francisco 'Italy without its art'; 'the mountains of California are so gigantic that they are not favour-
able to art or poetry'; Washington 'has too many bronze

generals'; and Chicago 'a sort of monster shop, full of bustle and bores'.

> When I was in America, I did not dare tell America the truth; but I saw it clearly even then – that the discovery of America was the beginning of the death of Art.
>
> (Quoted in Laurence Housman's *Echo de Paris*, 1923)

Wilde also took the opportunity to meet some of America's leading literary lights. Longfellow (1807–82) he wrote off as 'a great poet only for those who never read poetry'.

But of the legendary Walt Whitman (1819–92), Wilde wrote: 'I think him genuine, honest and manly', which was a strange use of words, since Whitman was a well-known homosexual.

> One of the first things I said was that he should call me 'Oscar'. 'I like that so much,' he answered, laying his hand on my knee.

Wilde paid Whitman the ultimate compliment by concluding that:

> There is something so Greek and sane about his poetry, it is so universal, so comprehensive. . . [he is] the closest approach to the Greek we have yet had in modern times.

He had much less time for Henry James (1843–1916). Admittedly, the relationship did not get off to the best of starts when Wilde – in an attempt to impress the novelist with his own sang-froid, exclaimed – 'You care for places? The world is *my* home.'

Wilde was later to remark that James wrote fiction 'as if it were a painful duty'. When his friends were canvassing the literary world for support during Wilde's later troubles, James was notable by the absence of his.

When the extended tour was over, Wilde was well pleased. He had already cabled home – GREAT SUCCESS HERE. NOTHING LIKE IT SINCE DICKENS. To his then friend, the painter James Whistler (1834–1903) he wrote:

> I have already civilised America – *Il reste seulement le ciel!*

Financially the tour had been less successful. The promoters made a profit of some £4,000 of which Wilde received £1,200. By the time he returned to England there was little of it left. None the less, he had achieved one of his main ambitions – he was now extremely well known for being famous on both sides of the Atlantic.

What seems to have gone largely unnoticed in America was that – probably because he had cloaked his remarks in somewhat impenetrable wit – Wilde's tour was a sustained attack on the materialistic vulgarity he saw dominating American society. He was for once not joking when he spoke of 'civilising America'.

> Their chilling touch is over everything. They are vulgarising mankind. The crude commercialism of America, its materialising spirit, its indifference to the poetical side of things,

and its lack of imagination and of high un-
attainable ideals, are entirely due to that
country having adopted for its national hero
a man who, according to his own confession,
was incapable of telling a lie.

(Related by Vivian in 'The Decay of Lying', who is then told
by Cyril that the story is a myth!)

In the mature plays, Wilde returns to the subject more play-
fully. American naïvety is frequently countered with
English sophistication. In *A Woman of No Importance*
(1893) in particular, he creates the opportunity by introduc-
ing the character of Miss Hester Worsley, a young lady visi-
tor from America:

HESTER: We have the largest country in
the world, Lady Caroline. They used to
tell us in school that some of our states
are as big as France and England put
together.

LADY CAROLINE: Ah! You must find it
very draughty...

LADY CAROLINE: There are a great many
things you haven't got in America, I am
told, Miss Worsley. They say you have no
ruins and no curiosities.

MRS ALLONBY: What nonsense! They
have their mothers and their manners.

(When he had tried the line out earlier in the story, 'The

Canterville Ghost', it had been 'your *navy* and your manners'.)

LADY HUNSTANTON: I don't know how he made his money originally.

KELVIL: I fancy in American dry goods.

LADY HUNSTANTON: What *are* American dry goods?

LORD ILLINGWORTH: American novels.

✒

MRS ALLONBY: They say, Lady Hunstanton, that when good Americans die, they go to Paris.

LADY HUNSTANTON: Indeed? And when bad Americans die, where do they go?

LORD ILLINGWORTH: Oh, they go to America.

✒

LORD ILLINGWORTH: The youth of America is their oldest tradition. It has been going on now for three hundred years. To hear them talk we would imagine they were in their first childhood. As far as civilisation goes they are in their second.

✒

LORD ILLINGWORTH: All Americans lecture, I believe. I suppose it is something in their climate.

In *The Picture of Dorian Gray*, Mr Erskine is advised that it is an 'education' to visit America:

> 'But must we really see Chicago to be
> educated?' asked Mr Erskine plaintively.
> 'I don't feel up to the journey.'

In the 1890s, in any case, the journey was increasingly in the other direction. London drawing rooms seemed to be increasingly populated by Miss Hester and her friends (suitably chaperoned, of course).

Once again, *A Woman of No Importance* provided a convenient platform:

> LADY CAROLINE: These American girls …
> Why can't they stay in their own country?
> They are always telling us it is the
> Paradise of women.
> LORD ILLINGWORTH: That is why they
> are so extremely anxious to get out of it.

> LADY CAROLINE (*to Hester*): It is not
> customary in England… for a young lady
> to speak with such enthusiasm of any
> person of the opposite sex. English
> women conceal their feelings until after
> they are married. They show them then.

> LORD HENRY: It is rather fashionable to
> marry Americans just now.

LORD FERMOR: I'll back English women
   against the world.
LORD HENRY: The betting is on the
   Americans.
LORD FERMOR: They don't last, I am told.
LORD HENRY: A long engagement
   exhausts them, but they are capital at a
   steeplechase.
(*The Picture of Dorian Gray*)

Wilde picked up the theme in his essays:

American women are bright, clever, and
wonderfully cosmopolitan. Their patriotic
feelings are limited to an admiration for
Niagara and a regret for the Elevated
Railway... They take their dresses from
Paris and their manners from Piccadilly, and
wear both charmingly... They insist on
being paid compliments and have almost
succeeded in making Englishmen eloquent
. . . in the art of amusing men they are adept,
both by nature and education, and can
actually tell a story without forgetting the
point – an accomplishment that is extremely
rare among the women of other countries...
On the whole the American invasion has
done English Society a great deal of good.
('The American Invasion')

Many American ladies on leaving their
native land adopt an appearance of chronic
ill-health, under the impression that it is a
form of European refinement. But Mrs Otis
had never fallen into that error… Indeed, in
many respects, she was quite English.

('The Canterville Ghost')

American girls are as clever at concealing
their parents as English women are at
concealing their past.

(Lord Henry Wotton in *The Picture of Dorian Gray*)

Drawing of Wilde in America with the artist's son,
by James Edward Kelly, 1882

Warned by the example of her mother that American women do not grow old gracefully, she tries not to grow old at all and often succeeds.

She behaves as if she was beautiful. Most American women do. It is the secret of their charm.
(Lord Henry Wotton in *The Picture of Dorian Gray*)

[American girls'] conversation sounds like a series of exploding crackers; they are exquisitely incoherent… the chief secret of their charm is that they never talk seriously except about amusements… [she] can talk brilliantly upon any subject, provided that she knows nothing about it.
('The American Invasion')

Every American girl is entitled to have twelve young men devoted to her. They remain her slaves and she rules them with charming nonchalance.
('Impressions of America')

BASIL HALLWARD: Marriage is hardly a thing that one can do now and then.

[*49*]

LORD HENRY WOTTON: Except in
America.
(*The Picture of Dorian Gray*)

His final verdict?

Pretty and charming – little oases of pretty
unreasonableness in a vast desert of
practical common sense.
(In conversation)

PART FIVE

Paris...
and Abroad

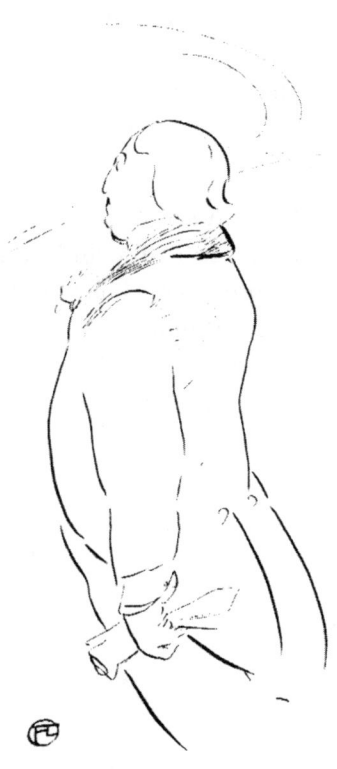

*'Oscar' by
Toulouse-Lautrec,
1895*

We are now concerned with the Oscar Wilde
of the second period, who has nothing whatever in common with the gentleman who
wore long hair and carried a sunflower down
Piccadilly.

(To Robert Sherard)

Paris ... the only civilised capital; the only
place on earth where you find absolute
toleration for all human frailties with
passionate admiration for all human virtues
and capacities.

(Conversation with Frank Harris)

You have never been to one of my parties...
I can't afford orchids, but I spare no expense
in foreigners. They make one's room look so
picturesque.

(Lady Wotton in *The Picture of Dorian Gray*)

No sooner had Wilde returned from America than he took himself off to Paris – the city which was to remain for him, in many ways, his spiritual home. He also took the occasion to re-invent his 'look'. Out went the velvet, the knee breeches and the silk stockings. He even took his Paris hairdresser with him to the Louvre and had him cut his hair after the style of a bust of Nero.

> One should either be a work of art, or wear a work of art.
>
> ('Phrases and Philosophies for the Use of the Young')

> Society must be amazed, and my Neronian coiffure has amazed it.

Always keen to comment on Wildean fashion, *Punch* carried an 'advertisement' for 'a large Stock of faded Lilies, dilapidated Sunflowers and shabby Peacocks' Feathers'. 'All that,' Wilde declared, 'belonged to the Oscar of the first period.'

Wilde was there ostensibly to write another play, *The Duchess of Padua* – which, like *Vera*, was not destined to find success – but his real purpose was to meet the men he considered his intellectual peers and establish his own credentials.

'There is,' he once noted, 'no modern literature outside France.' His great hero was Honoré de Balzac (1799–1850), whose *Comédie Humaine* was generally considered to be the archetype of the realistic novel.

> The nineteenth century, as we know it, is largely an invention of Balzac.
>
> ('The Decay of Lying')

He wrote in a review:

> It is pleasanter to have the *entrée* to his society than to receive cards from all the duchesses in Mayfair.

But the talents to which he found himself strangely drawn were the *décadents*: Charles-Pierre Baudelaire (1821–67), the scent of whose *Fleurs du Mal* lingered on; Stéphane Mallarmé (1842–98), leader of the Symbolist movement in poetry: and, particularly, the dissolute poet, Paul Verlaine (1844–96). Wilde was in Paris to dabble in decadence.

Unfortunately, the hero-worship was not always entirely reciprocated. The French critics – being French – prided themselves on their high academic standards and Wilde heard once more a complaint that had surfaced at the time of the publication of his *Poems* in 1881 – that they owed much to the work of others. (Wilde had sent one of the first copies to the Oxford Union Library. After due consideration, it was returned to him. A speaker at a Union debate claimed that they were 'for the most part... by William Shakespeare, by Philip Sidney, by John Donne, by Lord Byron, by William Morris, by Algernon Swinburne, and by sixty more'.)

Critic Edmond de Goncourt (1822–96) now went further and complained that Wilde was 'so given to plagiarising his fellow authors' that even his homosexuality was plagiarism of Verlaine's relationship with his lover, fellow poet Arthur Rimbaud (1854–91)

André Gide (1869–1951), later to become a good friend, was also less than impressed with the would-be 'High Priest of the Decadents'. Wilde, he claimed, did not converse, he narrated: 'He never listened and paid scant attention to ideas as soon as they were no longer his own. As soon as he ceased to shine all by himself, he effaced himself.'

None of which was allowed to throw Wilde off his stride. He came to admire and admire he did, mining every vein in sight to find things to satisfy him.

> The great superiority of France over England is that in France every *bourgeois* wants to be an artist, whereas in England every artist wants to be a *bourgeois*.
>
> (In conversation)

> While one is in London one hides everything; in Paris one reveals everything.
>
> (To a journalist)

> In Paris one can lose one's time most delightfully but one can never lose one's way.
>
> (In conversation)

Paris would remain the gold standard and it was not, by any means, for everyone. When his sometime friend, artist Aubrey Beardsley (1872–98) was out of favour:

> Dear Aubrey is almost *too* Parisian. He cannot forget that he has been to Dieppe – *once*.
>
> (Letter to Charles Ricketts)

The verbal construction so pleased him that he used it again on Frank Harris, who was listing the grand houses he had dined at:

> Dear Frank, we believe you; you have dined
> in every house in London – once.

Naturally, the differences he claimed to perceive between
the races would be turned to epigrammatic effect:

> Great men in France have loved women too
> much... In England great men love nothing,
> neither art, nor wealth, nor glory... nor
> women. It's an advantage, you can be sure.
> (Conversation with Louis Latourette)

Not that all Frenchmen were great men, not even all the
litérrateurs. The popular short story writer, Guy de
Maupassant (1850–93), for instance:

> strips life of the few poor rags that still cover
> her. He writes lurid little tragedies in which
> everybody is ridiculous; bitter comedies at
> which one cannot laugh for very tears.

Novelist Émile Zola (1840–1902) he decided:

> is determined to show that, if he has not got
> genius, he can at least be dull.

Paris – with its cultivated air of divine decay – was everything Wilde was determined it should be and the fact that
English society found it shocking (without ever trying to
understand it) made it even more attractive. From then on
he would use its 'decadence' as a point of literary reference.

In *Lady Windermere's Fan*, Mr Dumby describes the
infamous Mrs Erlynne as looking like ' an *édition de luxe* of
a wicked French novel, meant specially for the English

market'. And, in *A Woman of No Importance*, Lady Hunstanton makes the barbed comment about her contemporaries that 'most women in London, nowadays, seem to furnish their rooms with nothing but orchids, foreigners and French novels'.

In fact, Wilde felt so much at home in Paris that he even spoke French with an Irish brogue – something he never permitted himself when speaking London English.

From previous visits he had also learned to speak French colloquially enough to joke in it. At a party the conversation turned to the French Revolution and Marat, who met his well-deserved end by being drowned in his own bath tub.

C'est malheureux! [Wilde remarked]. *Il n'avait pas de veine – pour une fois qu'il a pris un bain!* (Poor devil, he was unlucky! To come to such grief for taking a bath for once!)

And to Frank Harris on the subject of the lugubrious Paris *gendarmes*:

Giving wrong directions to English tourists is the only thing that consoles them.

On one occasion, when English critics had particularly enraged him, he threatened to emigrate to Paris, where he was appreciated. The English press pointed out that if he did so, he might very well find himself the victim of the French army conscription system. *Punch* published a caricature of him dressed as a *poilu* (infantryman) in full marching gear.

[*57*]

A WILDE IDEA.
OR, MORE INJUSTICE TO IRELAND!

Punch *cartoon of Oscar as a* poilu, *1892*

In his later troubled years he professed to see in the French attitude all the understanding and compassion for the artist he had failed to find in England. In *De Profundis*, he claimed they understood that 'along with genius goes often a curious perversity of passion and desire'. What they could not comprehend was how the English could so treat 'an artist of my distinction, one who by the school and movement of which he was the incarnation had exercised a marked influence on the direction of French thought'.

The observation was Wilde's. Whether the French themselves would have endorsed the sentiment is open to question. When, after his release from prison, he went to Paris to die, his French followers were not exactly beating down his door.

Wilde travelled around Europe to some extent but most of his views on 'abroad' were his own invention.

The Germans held little appeal:

> The Rhine is, of course, tedious... as far as I can judge the inhabitants of Germany are Americans.
>
> (Letter to Robert Ross, 1899)

Presumably this was because most Germans were busy travelling themselves:

> Bosie was seated next to a German who exhaled in strange gusts the most extraordinary odours, some of them racial (it is smell that differentiates races); others connected with all kinds of trades from leather-dressing and carpentry to vitriol-works and

the keeping of an Italian warehouse…
others connected with gas, fuel and candles.
In the last act he became like a petroleum
lamp. Bosie bore it very well indeed: but had
practically to sit in my pocket.
(Letter to Robert Ross, 1898)

But I don't like German. It isn't at all a
becoming language. I know perfectly well I
look quite plain after my German lesson.
(Cecily in *The Importance of Being Earnest*)

Switzerland was not much better:

That dreadful place – so vulgar with its big
ugly mountains, all black and white like an
enormous photograph…

The Swiss are too ugly. I feel sure that the
reason they have produced nobody – but
theologians and waiters – is their lack of
physical beauty… their cattle have more
expression.
(Letter to Louis Wilkinson)

At one point in the early 1880s he had cherished an ambition to visit Japan…

where I will pass my youth, sitting under an
almond tree in white blossom, drinking

[60]

amber tea out of a blue cup, and looking at a landscape without perspective.

Later he revised his opinion:

The whole of Japan is pure invention. There is no such country, there are no such people... the Japanese people are... simply a mode of style, an exquisite fancy of art.

('The Decay of Lying')

Wilde never did visit Japan. Nor, for that matter, Australia, although something about the look of it fascinated him enough to refer to it more than once:

When I look at the map and see what an awfully ugly-looking country Australia is, I feel as if I want to go there to see if it cannot be changed into a more beautiful form.

(In conversation)

DUCHESS OF BERWICK: What a curious shape it is! Just like a large packing case. However, it is a very *young* country, isn't it?

MR HOPPER: Wasn't it made at the same time as the others, Duchess?

(*Lady Windermere's Fan*)

THIS ENGLAND...

Oscar Wilde by William Rothenstein, c. 1894

England is the home of lost ideas.

('The Decay of Lying')

Though I have English friends, I do not like the English in general. There is a great deal of hypocrisy in England...

(Interview with *Le Gaulois*)

Demmed clubs, demmed climate, demmed cooks, demmed everything. Sick of it all!

(Lord Augustus in *Lady Windermere's Fan*)

To WILDE everything was open to intellectual debate and a fair target for a correcting aphorism. What he never seemed to realise – or chose to ignore – was that the inhabitants of his adopted nation never care to be criticised on their own turf… and certainly not by a foreigner.

Wilde was too free and too consistent with his criticism of the English – and when the time came, too many of them remembered.

In 'The Critic As Artist':

Considered as an instrument of thought, the English mind is coarse and undeveloped… The English mind is always in a rage. The intellect of the race is wasted in the sordid and stupid quarrels of second-rate politicians or third-rate theologians.

Mediocrity weighing mediocrity in the balance, and incompetence applauding its brother – that is the spectacle which the artistic of England afford us from time to time.

England will never be civilised till she has added Utopia to her dominions.

There is no country so much in need of unpractical people as this country of ours.
[*Note the use of 'ours'.*]

> The real weakness of England lies... simply
> in the fact that her ideals are emotional and
> not intellectual.

And in 'The Soul of Man Under Socialism':

> In the present state of things in England, the
> people who do the most harm are the people
> who try to do most good... Charity creates a
> multitude of sins.

In 'The English Renaissance':

> Those things which the English public never
> forgives are youth, power, and enthusiasm.

By the time he had paid English society's price, of course, it
was not too surprising to find him writing to Georgina
Weldon in 1898 that:

> It is difficult to teach the English either pity
> or humanity. They learn slowly... It is the
> lack of imagination in the Anglo-Saxon race
> that makes the race so stupidly, harshly cruel.

But his most cutting diatribes came in his earlier years of
public acclaim:

> Remember to what a point your Puritanism
> in England has brought you. In old days
> nobody pretended to be a bit better than his
> neighbours. In fact, to be a bit better than
> one's neighbours was considered excessively

vulgar and middle-class.

(Mrs Cheveley in *An Ideal Husband*)

Lord Henry Wotton – Wilde's *doppelgänger* in *The Picture of Dorian Gray* – has a fine old time poking fun at his (*sic*) fellow Brits:

The British Race... represents the survival of the pushing.

A true Englishman... never dreams of considering whether the idea is right or wrong. The only thing he considers of any importance is whether one believes it oneself.

The British public are really not equal to the mental strain of having more than one topic every three months.

Ugliness is one of the seven deadly virtues... Beer, the Bible, and the seven deadly virtues have made our England what she is.

Englishmen... are more cunning than practical. When they make up their ledger, they balance stupidity by wealth, and vice by hypocrisy.

Great things have been thrust upon us and
we have carried their burden but only as far
as the Stock Exchange.

In this country it is enough for a man to have
distinction and brain for every common
tongue to wag against him... you forget that
we are in the native land of the hypocrite.
(Dorian in *The Picture of Dorian Gray*)

Hypocrisy was a favourite Wilde theme:

The typical Briton is Tartuffe, seated in his
shop behind the counter.

(Molière's eponymous hypocritical 'hero' was frequently
invoked.) When Lord Henry was asked what the Euro-
peans said of us, his reply was, 'Tartuffe has emigrated to
England and opened a shop.' Britain, the nation of shop-
keepers... In a notebook Wilde jotted: 'England – Caliban
for nine months of the year – Tartuffe for the other three.'

By the time of the plays, the bitterness had not abated
but the language had to be modified to a degree for public
consumption. In *An Ideal Husband*:

A typical Englishman, always dull and
usually violent.
(Mrs Cheveley)

Englishmen always get romantic after a
meal, and that bores me dreadfully.
(Mrs Cheveley)

The English can't stand a man who is
always saying he is right, but they are very
fond of a man who admits that he has been
in the wrong.

The English young lady is the dragon of
good taste.

(Vicomte de Nanjac in *An Ideal Husband*)

A dowdy, dull girl, with one of those
characteristic British faces, that, once seen,
are never remembered.

(*The Picture of Dorian Gray*)

The English think that a cheque book can
solve every problem in life.

(Mrs Cheveley in *An Ideal Husband*)

While his wit did not desert him, Wilde's sense of humour
on this particular topic frequently did:

Thinking is the most unhealthy thing in the
world, and people die of it just as they die of
any other disease. Fortunately, in England,
at any rate, thought is not catching.

('The Decay of Lying')

Our splendid physique as a people is entirely
due to our national stupidity.

⚜

Our stupidity, apparently, knew no bounds…

⚜

England… has invented and established
Public Opinion, which is an attempt to org-
anise the ignorance of the community, and to
elevate it to the dignity of physical force.
('The Critic As Artist')

⚜

Public opinion exists only where there are no
ideas.

⚜

The English are always degrading truths
into facts. When a truth becomes a fact it
loses all its intellectual value.
('A Few Maxims for the Instruction of the Over-Educated')

⚜

Certainly we are a degraded race, and have
sold our birthright for a mess of facts.
(Vivian in 'The Decay of Lying')

⚜

To disagree with three fourths of the British
public is one of the first elements of sanity.

As he told Frank Harris:

[70]

England is still only half-civilised; Englishmen touch life at one or two points without
suspecting its complexity. They are rude and
harsh.

The disillusion was deep-seated. As a student he had written in the *Dublin University Magazine* about... 'this dull
land of England, with its short summer, its dreary rains and
fogs, its mining districts, and factories, and vile deification
of machinery', but perhaps direct exposure to the phenome-
non eventually persuaded him the rapier of wit was more
effective than the bludgeon of confrontation.

I don't desire to change anything in England
except the weather.
(Lord Henry Wotton in *The Picture of Dorian Gray*)

There is something tragic about the
enormous number of young men there are in
England at the present moment who start
life with perfect profiles, and end by
adopting some useful profession.
('Phrases and Philosophies for the Use of the Young')

The island race were a safer target if one stuck to matters
that no self-respecting Englishman would consider important. Art, for instance...

England has more subjects for art than any
other country: I suppose that is the reason it
has fewer artists.
(Letter to Reggie Turner)

[*71*]

On the British intellect the illiterates play
the drum.
(Lord Illingworth in *A Woman of No Importance*)

⚗

That curious mixture of bad painting and
good intentions that always entitled a man
to be called a representative British artist.
(Lord Henry Wotton in *The Picture of Dorian Gray*)

... or poetry...

In England the Arts that have escaped best
are the arts in which the public take no
interest... We have been able to have fine
poetry... because the public do not read it,
and consequently do not influence it.
('The Soul of Man Under Socialism')

⚗

England never appreciates a poet until he is
dead.

⚗

... or fashion...

To be pretty is the best fashion there is, and
the only fashion England succeeds in setting.
(Lady Markby in *An Ideal Husband*)

And British cooking was always fair game, so to speak:

The British cook is a foolish woman – who
should be turned for her iniquities into a

[*72*]

pillar of salt, which she never knows how to use.

(In conversation)

There are twenty ways of cooking a potato and three hundred and sixty-five ways of cooking an egg, yet the British cook... knows only three methods of sending up either one or the other.

('Dinners and Dishes')

The English have a miraculous power to change wine into water.

(To Maurice Maeterlinck)

The complexities of London geography were always safe ground:

Bayswater is a place where people always get lost and there are no guides.

(In conversation)

West Kensington is a district to which you drive until the horse drops dead, when the cabman gets down and makes enquiries.

(In conversation)

And, of course, there was always the stalking horse of the *non*-British character in a play to make the point for you:

[73]

Oh, your English society seems to me shallow,
selfish, foolish. It has blinded its eyes, and
stopped its ears. It lies like a leper in purple…
(Hester in *A Woman of No Importance*)

You are unjust to women in England and
until you count what is a shame in a woman
to be infamy in a man, you will always be
unjust.
(Hester in *A Woman of No Importance*)

I guess the old country is so overpopulated
that they have not enough decent weather
for everybody. I have always been of the
opinion that emigration is the only thing for
England.
(American Minister in 'The Canterville Ghost')

Even the most revered British institutions were not spared.
Hunting provided one of Wilde's most quoted lines:

The English country gentleman galloping
after a fox – the unspeakable in full pursuit
of the uneatable.
(Lord Illingworth in *A Woman of No Importance*)

And of the British sense of humour:

Bosie has no real enjoyment of a joke unless
he thinks there is a good chance of the other

person being pained or annoyed. It is an
entirely English trait.
(Letter to Robert Ross, 1898)

It is only the dull who like practical jokes.
(In conversation)

If the cavemen had known how to laugh,
History would have been different.
(Lord Henry Wotton in *The Picture of Dorian Gray*)

And if Oscar Wilde had been a little more good-natured in
the way he poked fun at anything and everything English,
his own history might also have been different. What a real-
life Lord Augustus could say with impunity was not accept-
able from a weekend house guest.

LADY STUTFIELD: There is nothing, nothing
like the beauty of home-life, is there?
KELVIL: It is the mainstay of our moral system in England, Lady Stutfield. Without
it we would become like our neighbours.
(*A Woman of No Importance*)

How strange to live in a land where the
worship of beauty and the passion of love
are considered infamous. I hate England.
(To Alfred Douglas, November 1894)

Social Class

*Oscar, probably while lecturing
in Ireland, 1883*

Each class preaches the virtue of those virtues it need not exercise. The rich harp on the virtues of thrift, the idle grow eloquent over the dignity of labour.

(In conversation)

Work is the curse of the drinking classes.

(Attributed)

As a CARD-CARRYING member of London Society, Wilde began by adopting and to some degree satirising the views on the British social class system he found to be prevalent:

> I do not suppose that the criminal and illiterate classes ever read anything except newspapers.
>
> (Letter to the Editor of the *Scots Observer*, 1890)

> In London we have merely the ill-clad news-vendors, whose voice, in spite of the admirable efforts of the Royal College of Music to make England a really musical nation, is always out of tune, and whose rags, badly designed and badly worn, merely emphasise a painful note of uncomely misery, without conveying the impression of picturesqueness which is the only thing that makes the spectacle of the poverty of others at all bearable.
>
> (Letter to the Editor of *The Speaker*, 1891)

> As for the virtuous poor, one can pity them, of course, but one cannot possibly admire them.

And as for the middle class:

> Mrs Grundy, that amusing old lady... who represents the only original form of humour that the middle classes of this country have

been able to produce… The English public,
as a mass, takes no interest in a work of art
until it is told that the work in question is
immoral.

(Letter to the Editor of the *St James's Gazette*, 1890)

In his essays and earlier conversation, the tone was invariably patronising. He seemed to be discussing a race with which he had never come into contact. In 'The Soul of Man Under Socialism':

We are often told that the poor are grateful
for charity. Some of them are, no doubt,
but the best amongst the poor are never
grateful. They are ungrateful, discontented,
disobedient and rebellious. They are quite
right to be so.

✒

There is only one class in the community
that thinks more about money than the rich,
and that is the poor. The poor can think of
nothing else.

✒

The poor should be practical and prosaic.

('The Model Millionaire')

And even in his relatively late 'Phrases and Philosophies for the Use of the Young' (1894):

If the poor only had profiles there would be
no difficulty in solving the problems of
poverty.

[*80*]

As always, he found in his fiction a means of throwing his voice and putting his words into the mouths of others. But the raillery didn't change the dismissive nature of the underlying sentiment:

Really, if the lower orders don't set us a good example, what on earth is the use of them? They seem, as a class, to have absolutely no sense of moral responsibility.

(Algernon in *The Importance of Being Earnest*)

The people and their rights bore me... In these modern days to be vulgar, illiterate, common and vicious, seems to give a man a marvellous infinity of rights that his honest fathers never dreamed of.

(Prince Paul in *Vera, or The Nihilists*)

The masses feel that drunkenness, stupidity, and immorality should be their own special property, and that if any one of us makes an ass of himself, he is poaching on their preserves.

(Basil Hallward in *The Picture of Dorian Gray*)

MR KELVIL: I find that the poorer classes of this country display a marked desire for a higher ethical standard.

LADY STUTFIELD: How quite, quite nice of them.

(*A Woman of No Importance*)

We are over-charged for everything nowadays. I should fancy that the real tragedy of the poor is that they can afford nothing but self-denial.

(Lord Henry Wotton in *The Picture of Dorian Gray*)

It is only by not paying one's bills that one can hope to live in the memory of the commercial classes.

('Phrases and Philosophies for the Use of the Young')

Three addresses always inspire confidence, even in tradesmen.

(Lady Bracknell in *The Importance of Being Earnest*)

Once, riding on an omnibus, Wilde found himself without the fare. Nor could any of the other passengers be prevailed upon to provide it. In high dudgeon, he descended and hailed a cab, in the confidence that the people he was visiting would pay for it.

People have more confidence in someone who takes a cab than in someone who uses a public conveyance.

It is vulgar to talk like a dentist when one isn't a dentist. It produces a false impression.

(Jack in *The Importance of Being Earnest*)

CECILY: When I see a spade I call it a spade.

GWENDOLEN: I am glad to say that I have never seen a spade. It is obvious that our social spheres have been widely different.

(*The Importance of Being Earnest*)

LADY BASILDON: Ah! I hate being educated!

MRS MARCHMONT: So do I. It puts one almost on a level with the commercial classes.

(*An Ideal Husband*)

LORD GORING: Extraordinary thing about the lower classes in England – they are always losing their relations.

(*An Ideal Husband*)

And on the subject of happy marriages:

MRS ALLONBY: Oh, they are quite out of date.

LADY STUTFIELD: Except among the
middle classes, I have been told.
MRS ALLONBY: How like the middle classes.
(*A Woman of No Importance*)

Good works on the part of the upper classes came in for
their share of comment:

They're always at the window doing fancy
work, and making ugly things for the poor,
which I think is so useful of them in these
dreadful Socialistic days.
(Duchess of Berwick in *Lady Windermere's Fan*)

I don't quite like women who are interested
in Philanthropic work. I think it is so forward
of them.
(Cecily in *The Importance of Being Earnest*)

Prison brought Wilde a new and more realistic perspective.
By the time he was released, he had learned to despise high
society and loathe the values of the 'ordinary people' who
made up the middle class:

The intellectual and emotional life of ordinary people is a very contemptible affair. Just
as they borrow their ideas from a sort of
circulating library of thought – the Zeitgeist
of an age that has no soul – and send them
back soiled at the end of each week, so they
always try to get their emotions on credit,

and refuse to pay the bill when it comes in.
(*De Profundis*)

The poor are wiser, more charitable, more
kind, more sensitive than we are.
(*De Profundis*)

Which did not render them safe from comment. However,
Wilde's last recorded remark on the subject had a twinkle
in its eye. Writing in 1898 to his publisher, Leonard Smithers, concerning the publication of 'The Ballad of Reading
Gaol', he came up with a novel suggestion for marketing it:

As I want the poem to reach the poorer
classes, we might give away a cake of Maypole
soap with each copy: I hear it dyes people
the most lovely colours, and is also cleansing.

MANNERS, MORALS AND MORES

Oscar as An Ideal Husband, 1894

Never speak disrespectfully of Society...
only people who can't get into it do that.
(Lady Bracknell in *The Importance of Being Earnest*)

✍

I think that life is far too important a thing
ever to talk seriously about it.
(Lord Darlington in *Lady Windermere's Fan*)

✍

I have the simplest tastes. I am always
satisfied with the best.
(In conversation)

✍

London Society... is entirely composed of
beautiful idiots and brilliant lunatics. Just
what Society should be!
(Mabel Chiltern in *An Ideal Husband*)

SOCIETY:

> To be in it is merely a bore. But to be out of it
> is simply a tragedy. Society is a necessary
> thing.
>
> (Lord Illingworth in *A Woman of No Importance*)

Society was Oscar Wilde's objective. Once he had gained it, it rapidly became his undoing. At no time, though, did he have any illusions about it: 'a lot of damned nobodies talking about nothing' – as Lord Caversham describes it in *An Ideal Husband*.

> MRS MARCHMONT: London Society is
> entirely made up of dowdies and dandies.
> LORD GORING: The men are all dowdies
> and the women are all dandies, aren't
> they?

> Society, civilised Society at least, is never
> very ready to believe anything to the
> detriment of those who are both rich and
> fascinating... [it] feels instinctively that
> manners are of more importance than
> morals, and, in its opinion, the highest
> respectability is of no less value than the
> possession of a good chef.
>
> (*The Picture of Dorian Gray*)

The 'manners and morals' remark would turn out to be at the heart of the case Society built against him. Like so many of his epigrams, it turned out to be retrospectively prophetic.

In my young days… one never met anyone
in society who worked for his living. It was
not considered the thing.

(Lady Caroline in *A Woman of No Importance*)

I have often observed that the Season as it
goes on produces a kind of softening of the
brain.

(Lady Markby in *An Ideal Husband*)

The most important consolation that women
find in modern life is taking someone else's
admirer when one loses one's own. In good
society that always whitewashes a woman.

(Lord Henry Wotton in *The Picture of Dorian Gray*)

To get into the best society nowadays, one
has either to feed people, amuse people, or
shock people – that is all!

Talk to every woman as if you loved her,
and to every man as if he bored you, and at
the end of the first season you will have the
reputation of possessing the most perfect
social tact.

No man has any real success in this world
unless he has got women to back him, and
women rule society.

(In conversation)

✍

A man who can dominate a London dinner-
table can dominate the world. The future
belongs to the dandy. It is the exquisites who
are going to rule.

(Lord Illingworth in *A Woman of No Importance*)

✍

The London Season!… People are either
hunting for husbands or hiding from them.

(Mrs Cheveley in *An Ideal Husband*)

✍

GERALD: There are many different kinds
of women, aren't there?

LORD ILLINGWORTH: Only two kinds in
society; the plain and the coloured.

GERALD: But there are good women in
society, aren't there?

LORD ILLINGWORTH: Far too many.

(*A Woman of No Importance*)

✍

After a good dinner one forgives anybody,
even one's own relations.

(Lady Caroline in *A Woman of No Importance*)

The clever people never listen, and the stupid people never talk.

(Mrs Allonby in *A Woman of No Importance*)

The well-bred contradict other people. The wise contradict themselves.

('Phrases and Philosophies for the Use of the Young')

The basis of the stability of society, as a healthy society, is the complete absence of any intelligence among its members.

('The Critic As Artist')

He must be quite respectable. One has never heard his name before in the whole course of one's life, which speaks volumes for a man, nowadays.

(Lady Caroline in *A Woman of No Importance*)

Wilde himself had no doubt that the stability of society also depended on following certain understood guidelines, which even he would not flout:

If I were all alone marooned on a desert island and I had my things with me, I should dress for dinner every evening.

(In conversation)

Arguments are extremely vulgar, for

everybody in good society holds exactly the same opinions.

(The Frog in 'The Remarkable Rocket')

The mind of a thoroughly well-informed man is a dreadful thing. It is like a bric-à-brac shop, all monsters and dust, with everything priced above its proper value.

(Lord Henry Wotton in *The Picture of Dorian Gray*)

Of course, one must never forget that the whole thing was a complex but endlessly charming charade:

What is interesting about people in good society is the mask that each one of them wears, not the reality that lies behind the mask.

('The Decay of Lying')

The mask was to become a recurring image:

Give a man a mask and he will tell you the truth.

A mask tells us more than a face.

('Pen, Pencil and Poison')

Only in mirrors is it well to look, for mirrors do but show us masks.

(Herod in *Salomé*)

Wilde's own mask was the one of studied superficiality:

> To the world I seem by intention on my part,
> a dilettante and dandy merely – it is not wise
> to show one's heart to the world – and as
> seriousness of manner is the disguise of the
> fool, folly in its exquisite modes of triviality
> and indifference and lack of care is the robe
> of the wise man. In so vulgar an age as this
> we all need masks.
>
> (Letter to Philip Houghton, 1894)

Even in prison it became a necessity more than a device:

> Those who want a mask have to wear it.
>
> (Letter to Philip Houghton, 1894)

And there were many who played the game and lost:

> [Lady Brandon] tried to found a *salon* and
> only succeeded in opening a restaurant.
>
> (Lord Henry Wotton in *The Picture of Dorian Gray*)

(This is another example of Wilde polishing a line. Five years or so earlier an acquaintance, André Raffalovich, 'came to London to start a *salon* and has only succeeded in opening a saloon'.)

The only players who really counted on the card were the aristocracy:

> The Peerage is the one book a young man
> about town should know thoroughly and it
> is the best thing in fiction the English have
> ever done.
>
> (Lord Illingworth in *A Woman of No Importance*)

There is always more brass than brains in an aristocracy.

(Prince Paul in *Vera, or The Nihilists*)

A title is really rather a nuisance in these democratic days. As George Harford I had everything I wanted. Now I have merely everything that other people want.

(Lord Illingworth in *A Woman of No Importance*)

Credit is the capital of a younger son and one lives charmingly upon it.

(Lord Henry Wotton in *The Picture of Dorian Gray*)

Very occasionally – and usually under duress – one of the players would drop out of the game and have to rationalise that decision:

London is too full of fogs – and serious people. Whether the fogs produce the serious people or whether the serious people produce the fogs, I don't know, but the whole thing rather gets on my nerves.

(Mrs Erlynne in *Lady Windermere's Fan*)

The fact is that our Society is terribly over-populated. Really, someone should arrange a proper scheme of assisted emigration.

(Lady Markby in *An Ideal Husband*)

To ask the rules of London Society was proof positive that one could not possibly be part of it. Yet unwritten rules there certainly were – as rigidly laid down as the London tramway system. Wilde had great fun satirising them and making up new Dos and Don'ts of his own. There was Wilde's Law of Triviality:

It is only shallow people who do not judge by appearances.

(Lord Henry Wotton in *The Picture of Dorian Gray*)

Only the shallow know themselves.

('Phrases and Philosophies for the Use of the Young')

It is only the superficial qualities that last. Man's deeper qualities are soon found out.

(Cecily in *The Importance of Being Earnest*)

Not that those 'deeper qualities' are necessarily any more admirable:

Charity creates a multitude of sins.

('The Soul of Man Under Socialism')

Philanthropic people lose all sense of humanity. It is their distinguishing characteristic.

(Lord Henry Wotton in *The Picture of Dorian Gray*)

Philanthropy seems to me to have become

simply the refuge of people who wish to
annoy their fellow creatures.
(Mrs Cheveley in *An Ideal Husband*)

I am afraid that good people do a great deal
of harm in the world... It is absurd to divide
people into good and bad. People are either
charming or tedious.
(Lord Darlington in *Lady Windermere's Fan*)

All charming people, I fancy, are spoiled. It
is the secret of their attraction.
(*The Portrait of Mr W. H.*)

Then there were the Wilde Rules for Survival and Success
in Society:

One should always play fairly – when one
has the winning cards.
(Mrs Cheveley in *An Ideal Husband*)

It is always nice to be expected and not to
arrive.
(Lord Goring in *An Ideal Husband*)

To be premature is to be perfect.
('Phrases and Philosophies for the Use of the Young')

To be natural is such a very difficult pose to keep up.

(Mrs Cheveley in *An Ideal Husband*)

✦

Only dull people are brilliant at breakfast.

(Mrs Cheveley in *An Ideal Husband*)

✦

Never buy a thing you don't want merely because it is dear.

(In conversation)

✦

I never put off until tomorrow what I can possibly do – the day after.

(In conversation)

✦

Of course, for Wilde the real social art was the Art of Conversation:

Conversation should touch everything but should concentrate on nothing.

('The Critic As Artist')

✦

Lots of people act well but very few people talk well, which shows that talking is much more the difficult thing of the two.

('The Devoted Friend')

✦

Nowadays to talk intelligibly is to be found out.

(Lord Darlington in *Lady Windermere's Fan*)

If one tells the truth, one is sure, sooner or later, to be found out.

('Phrases and Philosophies for the Use of the Young')

That observation... has all the vitality of error and all the tediousness of an old friend.

('The Critic As Artist')

She doesn't care much for eloquence in others. She thinks it a little loud.

(Lord Goring in *An Ideal Husband*)

[She] talks more and says less than anybody I ever met. She is made to be a public speaker.

(Mrs Cheveley in *An Ideal Husband*)

He talks the whole time. But he has got no conversation.

(Mrs Allonby in *A Woman of No Importance*)

Questions are never indiscreet. Answers sometimes are.

(Mrs Cheveley in *An Ideal Husband*)

It is always worthwhile asking a question. It is not always worthwhile answering one.

(Lord Goring in *An Ideal Husband*)

I don't propose to talk about modern culture. It isn't the sort of thing one should talk about in private.

(Jack in *The Importance of Being Earnest*)

It is very vulgar to talk about one's business. Only people like stockbrokers do that, and then merely at dinner parties.

(Algernon in *The Importance of Being Earnest*)

Whenever people talk to me about the weather, I always feel quite certain that they mean something else.

(Gwendolen in *The Importance of Being Earnest*)

How clever you are, my dear! You never mean a single word you say.

(Lady Hunstanton in *A Woman of No Importance*)

One should never listen. To listen is a sign of
indifference to one's hearers.

('A Few Maxims for the Instruction of the Over-Educated')

I like looking at geniuses, and listening to
beautiful people!

(Mrs Marchmont in *An Ideal Husband*)

Actions are the first tragedy in life, words
are the second. Words are perhaps the worst.
Words are merciless.

(Lady Windermere in *Lady Windermere's Fan*)

After all, the only proper intoxication is
conversation.

(Letter from Paris, May 1898)

'Mr Punch's Fairy Tale Christmas Cards', 1881

[*101*]

In each of the first three 'Society' plays, Wilde inhabits the character of the aristocratic reprobate who – because of his social position – can utter scandalous remarks about the group of which he is a privileged insider.

Many critics have been tempted to see the plays – and their precursor, the novel *The Picture of Dorian Gray* – as simply drawing-room comedies and vehicles for Wilde's wit. Closer examination reveals them to be highly subversive commentaries of the fundamental insecurities of a social structure desperately trying to shore itself up against inevitable social and political change. The enemy was also within and leading the infiltration was – Oscar Wilde.

Lord Illingworth in *A Woman of No Importance*, Lord Darlington in *Lady Windermere's Fan* and Lord Goring in *An Ideal Husband* all act as *agents provocateurs* but easily the most dangerous (because the least charming) is Lord Henry Wotton in *Dorian Gray*. A montage of his misanthropic social observations gives something of the flavour:

I like persons better than principles and I like persons with no principles better than anything in the world… Whenever a man does a thoroughly stupid thing, it is always from the noblest motives… I adore simple pleasures. They are the last refuge of the complex… No civilised man ever regrets a pleasure, and no uncivilised man knows what a pleasure is… The only thing one never regrets are one's mistakes… I can believe anything, provided that it is quite incredible… Good resolutions are useless

attempts to interfere with scientific laws –
they are simply cheques that men draw on a
bank where they have no account. One can
always be kind to people about whom one
cares nothing... The man who could call a
spade a spade should be compelled to use
one. It is the only thing he is fit for... Every
effect that one produces gives one an enemy.
To be popular one must be a mediocrity...
One has a right to judge a man by the effect
he has over his friends... Laughter is not at
all a bad thing for a friendship, and it is by
far the best ending for one.

Lord Henry's friends, it would seem, could never be sure of
seeing him until he actually appeared:

I am prevented from coming in consequence
of a subsequent engagement.

As he might have observed to Dorian Gray:

Pleasure is the only thing one should live for.
Nothing ages like happiness.
('Phrases and Philosophies For the Use of the Young')

Not that Lord Henry had cornered the market in bad
behaviour. 'Wickedness', real or affected, continued to fas-
cinate Wilde:

Wickedness is a myth invented by good

people to account for the curious attractive-
ness of others.

('Phrases and Philosophies for the Use of the Young')

If you pretend to be good, the world takes
you very seriously. If you pretend to be bad,
it doesn't… There are some people who say
I have never really done anything wrong in
the whole course of my life. Of course, they
only say it behind my back.

(Lord Darlington in *Lady Windermere's Fan*)

It is perfectly monstrous the way people go
about nowadays, saying things against one
behind one's back that are absolutely and
entirely true.

(Lord Illingworth in *A Woman of No Importance*)

I hope that you have not been leading a
double life, pretending to be wicked and
being really good all the time. That would
be hypocrisy.

(Cecily in *The Importance of Being Earnest*)

It is a terrible thing for a man to find out
suddenly that all his life he has been
speaking nothing but the truth.

(Jack in *The Importance of Being Earnest*)

The man who regards his past is a man who deserves to have no future to look forward to.
('The Critic As Artist')

One should believe evil of everyone, until, of course, people are found out to be good.
(Lady Caroline in *A Woman of No Importance*)

To have friends... one need only be good-natured: but when a man has no enemy left there must be something mean about him.
(Prince Paul in *Vera, or The Nihilists*)

I choose my friends for their good looks, my acquaintances for their good characters, and my enemies for their good intellects. A man cannot be too careful in the choice of his enemies.
(Lord Henry Wotton in *The Picture of Dorian Gray*)

You have wonderfully good taste, Ernest... It's the excuse I've always given for leading such a bad life.
(Cecily in *The Importance of Being Earnest*)

In prison he was taking a more sombre view:

Most people are other people. Their thoughts

are someone else's opinions, their lives a
mimicry, their passions a quotation.

(*De Profundis*, 1897)

The word 'Gentleman' was to recur frequently. Precisely
what *was* a Gentleman? Well, there were a number of tiny
clues:

No gentleman ever takes exercise. You don't
seem to understand what a gentleman is.

(Algernon in *The Importance of Being Earnest*)

No gentleman dines before seven.

(Lord Henry Wotton in *The Picture of Dorian Gray*)

A gentleman never goes east of Temple Bar.

(In conversation)

When the proprietor of a hotel was inviting Wilde to look
out of his hotel window at the splendid view:

Oh, that is altogether immaterial… a
gentleman never looks out of the window.

How perfectly silly you are. No gentleman
ever has any money.

(Algernon in *The Importance of Being Earnest*)

No gentleman ever corroborates anything.
(Jack in *The Importance of Being Earnest*)

One of Nature's gentlemen, the worst type
of gentleman I know.
(In conversation)

The man who sees both sides of a question is
a man who sees absolutely nothing at all.
('The Critic As Artist')

We always used to say of him that he would
be the best of fellows, if he did not always
speak the truth.
(Lord Murchison in 'The Sphinx Without a Secret')

For even the best-intentioned there were snares every step
of the way:

I have known men come to London full of
bright prospects and see them complete
wrecks in a few months through the habit of
answering letters.
(Letter to Arthur Fish, Assistant Publisher of *Woman's World*)

A 'Lady' also required precise definition:

A poor woman who is not straight is a
prostitute, but a rich one is a lady of fashion.
(In conversation)

Then there is the whole question of style. After all, we are
what we eat and wear:

> Give me the luxuries and anyone can have
> the necessities.
>
> (In conversation with Frank Harris)

In matters of grave importance, style, not
sincerity, is the vital thing.

(Gwendolen in *The Importance of Being Earnest*)

'Fashion is what one wears oneself,' said Lord Goring in
An Ideal Husband, who then went on to lecture his man-
servant, Phipps:

> What is unfashionable is what other people
> wear… Just as vulgarity is simply the
> conduct of other people… and falsehoods
> the truth of other people… Other people are
> quite dreadful. The only possible society is
> oneself… To love oneself is the beginning of
> a lifelong romance.

Fashion, by which what is really fantastic
becomes for a moment universal.

(*The Picture of Dorian Gray*)

A fashion is merely a form of ugliness so

unbearable that we are compelled to alter it
every six months.

A well-tied tie is the first serious step in life.
(Lord Illingworth in *A Woman of No Importance*)

A really well-made buttonhole is the only
link between Art and Nature.
('Phrases and Philosophies for the Use of the Young')

A line that Wilde liked enough to use three times with
minor variations was:

He atones for being occasionally somewhat
over-dressed by being always absolutely
over-educated.
(Lord Henry Wotton in *The Picture of Dorian Gray*)

Dandyism is the assertion of the absolute
modernity of Beauty.
('A Few Maxims for the Instruction of the Over-Educated')

With an evening coat and a white tie...
anybody, even a stockbroker, can gain a
reputation for being civilised.
(Basil Hallward in *The Picture of Dorian Gray*)

When in doubt, Wilde was invariably inclined to pin the
Order of Bad Taste on the unfortunate stockbroker. Female

fashion, of course, had its own arcane rules:

> All good hats are made out of nothing.
> (Duchess of Monmouth in *The Picture of Dorian Gray*)

Wilde claimed that he once saw in a French magazine a picture of a lady's Bonnet with the caption:

> With this style the mouth is worn slightly open.

Which perhaps inspired:

> Style largely depends on the way the chin is worn. They are worn very high, just at present.
> (Lady Bracknell in *The Importance of Being Earnest*)

> JACK: I must admit I smoke.
> LADY BRACKNELL: A man should always have an occupation of some kind.
> (*The Importance of Being Earnest*)

Wilde himself was a heavy smoker, even though he only took a few puffs before moving on to the next one. They were invariably gold-tipped.

> A cigarette is the perfect type of a perfect pleasure. It is exquisite, and it leaves one unsatisfied. What more can one want?
> (Lord Henry Wotton in *The Picture of Dorian Gray*)

> Gold-tipped cigarettes are awfully expensive.

I can only afford them when I'm in debt.

(Lord Alfred in *A Woman of No Importance*)

Half the pretty women in London smoke
cigarettes. Personally, I prefer the other half.

(Lord Goring in *An Ideal Husband*)

I have made an important discovery...
that alcohol, taken in sufficient quantities,
produces all the effects of intoxication.

(In conversation)

With certain exceptions, Wilde's favourite absinthe being
one...

After the first glass you see things as you
wish they were. After the second you see
things as they are not. Finally you see things
as they really are and that is the most
horrible thing in the world.

(Conversation with Ada Leverson)

All too often at a fashionable dinner party the ladies were
too long in retiring. Before they did so, there was no opportunity for the gentlemen to smoke. On one particularly frustrating occasion the hostess happened to notice that a
lampshade was smouldering. 'Please put it out, Mr Wilde –
it's smoking.' 'Happy lamp!' Wilde is supposed to have
murmured. As for the meal which preceded the remark, we
know nothing of it except that it would certainly have been
prepared with considerable care:

Even the cardinal virtues cannot atone for half-cold *entrées*.

(*The Picture of Dorian Gray*)

I hate people who are not serious about meals. It is so shallow of them.

(Algernon in *The Importance of Being Earnest*)

Wilde advertising cigars on a US trade card, 1882

Cake is rarely seen at the best houses now-adays.

(Gwendolen in *The Importance of Being Earnest*)

When I ask for a watercress sandwich, I do not mean a loaf with a field in the middle of it.

(Quoted in a letter from Max Beerbohm to Reginald Turner, 15 April 1883)

By a complex convolution of the plot and a multiple confusion of identities, Algernon is about to be arrested for not paying an hotel bill and complains:

> Holloway! Well, I really am not going to be imprisoned in the suburbs for having dinner in the West End. It is perfectly ridiculous!
>
> (Algernon in *The Importance of Being Earnest*)

It is one more of Wilde's lines that proved pre-emptive.

Sprouting like some exotic plants throughout his work are Wilde's Eternal Social Truths.

TEMPTATION

> Life's aim, if it has one, is simply to be always looking for temptations. There are not nearly enough. I sometimes pass a whole day without coming across a single one.
>
> (Lord Illingworth in *A Woman of No Importance*)

> I can resist everything except temptation.
>
> (Lord Darlington in *Lady Windermere's Fan*)

> The only way to get rid of a temptation is to yield to it. Resist it and the soul grows sick.
>
> (Lord Henry Wotton in *The Picture of Dorian Gray*)

There are terrible temptations that it
requires strength, strength and courage to
yield to.

(Sir Robert Chiltern in *An Ideal Husband*)

The capacity of yielding to temptations is
the test of one's character... Only the weak
resist temptation.

(Attributed)

Lady Windermere and the Duchess of Paisley are discussing palmistry in which Lady Windermere believes
devoutly:

DUCHESS OF PAISLEY: But surely that is
tempting Providence, Gladys.

LADY WINDERMERE: My dear Duchess,
surely Providence can resist temptation
by this time.

('Lord Arthur Savile's Crime')

SINCERITY

A little sincerity is a dangerous thing, and a
great deal of it is absolutely fatal.

('The Critic As Artist')

Insincerity... is merely a method by which
we can multiply our personalities.

(Lord Henry Wotton in *The Picture of Dorian Gray*)

CYNICISM

> A cynic... is a man who knows the price of
> everything and the value of nothing.
>
> (Lord Darlington in *Lady Windermere's Fan*)

> To the true cynic nothing is ever revealed.
>
> (In conversation)

> JACK: For heaven's sake, don't try to be
> cynical. It's perfectly easy to be cynical.
> ALGERNON: My dear fellow, it isn't easy to
> be anything nowadays. There's such a lot
> of beastly competition about.
>
> (*The Importance of Being Earnest*)

PHILOSOPHY

> THE ROCKET: I often have long
> conversations with myself, and I am so
> clever that sometimes I don't understand
> a single word of what I am saying.
> THE DRAGON-FLY: Then you should
> certainly lecture on Philosophy.
>
> ('The Remarkable Rocket')

MONEY

> I don't want money. It is only people who
> pay their bills who want that, and I never
> pay mine.
>
> (Lord Henry Wotton in *The Picture of Dorian Gray*)

MORALITY

Morality is simply the attitude we adopt towards people whom we personally dislike.

(Mrs Cheveley in *An Ideal Husband*)

Any preoccupation with ideas of what is right or wrong in conduct shows an arrested intellectual development.

Early in life she had discovered the important truth that nothing looks so like innocence as an indiscretion.

(Said of Lady Windermere in 'Lord Arthur Savile's Crime')

Gossip is charming!… But scandal is gossip made tedious by morality.

(Cecil Graham in *Lady Windermere's Fan*)

The basis for any scandal is an immoral certainty.

(Lord Henry Wotton in *The Picture of Dorian Gray*)

I love scandals about other people, but scandals about myself don't interest me. They have not got the charm of novelty.

(Dorian in *The Picture of Dorian Gray*)

Scandals used to lend charm, or at least interest, to a man – now they crush him.

One should never make one's début with a scandal. One should reserve that to give an interest to one's old age.

(Lord Henry Wotton in *The Picture of Dorian Gray*)

EXPERIENCE

Experience is the name everyone gives to their mistakes.

(Mr Dumby in *Lady Windermere's Fan*)

Experience is a question of instinct about life.

(In conversation)

I myself would sacrifice everything for a new experience, and I know that there is no such thing as a new experience at all.

(1886)

MODERATION

Moderation is a fatal thing... Nothing succeeds like excess.

(Lord Illingworth in *A Woman of No Importance*)

When he used the same line with Lord Henry in *The Picture of Dorian Gray* he ended it:

Enough is as bad as a meal. More than enough is as good as a feast.

Ｘ

People who count their chickens before they are hatched, act very wisely, because chickens run about so absurdly that it is impossible to count them accurately.

SUFFERING

I can sympathise with everything except suffering… The less said about life's sores the better.

(Lord Henry Wotton in *The Picture of Dorian Gray*)

EXCESS

Anything becomes a pleasure if one does it too often.

STUPIDITY

There is no sin except stupidity.

('The Critic As Artist')

Ｘ

There is more to be said for stupidity than people imagine.

(Lord Goring in *An Ideal Husband*)

Ｘ

The only thing that ever consoles man for the stupid things he does is the praise he always gives himself for doing them.

(In conversation)

ADVICE

It is always a silly thing to give advice, but to give good advice is absolutely fatal.

(*The Portrait of Mr W. H.*)

Pick-Me-Up *magazine shows Oscar as 'A Voluptuary', 1894*

LORD GORING: I am going to give you some good advice.

MRS CHEVELEY: Oh, pray don't. One should never give a woman anything she can't wear in the evening.

(*An Ideal Husband*)

I always pass on good advice. It is the only thing to do with it. It is never of any use to oneself.

(Lord Goring in *An Ideal Husband*)

People are very fond of giving away what they need most themselves. It is what I call the depth of generosity.

(Lord Henry Wotton in *The Picture of Dorian Gray*)

It is only about things which do not interest one that one can give a really unbiased opinion, which is no doubt the reason why an unbiased opinion is always absolutely valueless.

('The Critic As Artist')

WORK

Hard work is simply the refuge of people who have nothing whatever to do.

('The Remarkable Rocket')

Man is made for something better than
disturbing dirt.
('The Soul of Man Under Socialism')

To do nothing at all is the most difficult
thing in the world, the most difficult and the
most intellectual.
('The Critic As Artist')

It is awfully hard work doing nothing.
However, I don't mind hard work where
there is no definite object of any kind.
(Algernon in *The Importance of Being Earnest*)

It is a great advantage to have done nothing,
but not one to be exploited.

And, of course, Lord Fermor in *The Picture of Dorian Gray*
was introduced as master of 'the great aristocratic art of
doing absolutely nothing'.

Work never seems to me a reality, but a way
of getting rid of reality.
(Letter to W. E. Henley)

Industry is the root of all ugliness.
('Phrases and Philosophies for the Use of the Young')

HESITATION
Hesitation of any kind is a sign of mental

decay in the young, of physical weakness in the old.

(Lady Bracknell in *The Importance of Being Earnest*)

DUTY

Duty is what one expects from others, it is not what one does oneself.

(Lord Illingworth in *A Woman of No Importance*)

My duty is a thing I never do, on principle.

(Lord Goring in *An Ideal Husband*)

RELATIONS

Relations are simply a tedious pack of people, who haven't the remotest knowledge of how to live, nor the smallest instinct about when to die.

Relations never lend one any money, and won't give one credit even for genius. They are a sort of aggravated form of the public.

(Algernon in *The Importance of Being Earnest*)

I can't help detesting my relations. I suppose it comes from the fact that none of us can stand other people having the same faults as ourselves.

(Lord Henry Wotton in *The Picture of Dorian Gray*)

No one cares about distant relations nowadays. They went out of fashion years ago.

('Lord Arthur Savile's Crime')

CHARITY

Charity dear Miss Prism, charity! None of us
are perfect. I myself am peculiarly susceptible
to draughts.

(Canon Chasuble in *The Importance of Being Earnest*)

INDIFFERENCE

Indifference is the revenge the world takes
on mediocrities.

(Prince Paul in *Vera, or The Nihilists*)

You like everyone; that is to say, you are
indifferent to everyone.

(Basil Hallward in *The Picture of Dorian Gray*)

TAXES

When he received a tax demand, Wilde asked why he
should pay.

TAX COLLECTOR: But you are the house-
holder here, are you not? You live here,
you sleep here.

WILDE: Ah, yes; but then I sleep so badly!

CONSCIENCE

Conscience and cowardice are really the
same things… Conscience is the trade-name
of the firm. That is all.

(Lord Henry Wotton in *The Picture of Dorian Gray*)

SENTIMENT

I cannot repeat an emotion; no one can except sentimentalists.

(Dorian in *The Picture of Dorian Gray*)

A sentimentalist is simply one who desires to have the luxury of an emotion without paying for it.

(In conversation)

Sentimentality is merely the bank holiday of cynics.

(Attributed)

A sensitive person is one who, because he has corns himself, always treads on other people's toes.

('The Remarkable Rocket')

TIME

Punctuality is the thief of time.

(In conversation)

Time is a waste of money.

('Phrases and Philosophies for the Use of the Young')

THOUGHT

All thought is immoral. Its very essence is destruction. If you think of anything, you

kill it. Nothing survives being thought of.
(Lord Illingworth in *A Woman of No Importance*)

GOODNESS

When we are happy we are always good but
when we are good we are not always happy.

To be good is to be in harmony with oneself.
Discord is to be forced to be in harmony
with others.
(In conversation)

There is a fatality about all good resolutions.
They are invariably made too soon.
('Phrases and Philosophies for the Use of the Young')

FRIENDSHIP

Friendship is more tragic than love. It lasts
longer.
('A Few Maxims for the Instruction of the Over-Educated')

GENIUS

Not being a genius, he had no enemies.
('Lord Arthur Savile's Crime')

The worst thing you can do for a person of
genius is to help him: that way lies his
destruction. I have had many devoted
helpers – and you see the result.
(In conversation)

POVERTY

The only thing that can console one for being poor is extravagance.

The only thing that can console one for being rich is economy.

('A Few Maxims for the Instruction of the Over-Educated')

Wilde, it must be said, followed the first precept to the very end of his life but there is no evidence that in his period of relative wealth he took the slightest bit of notice of the second.

TRUTH

A truth ceases to be a truth when more than one person believes in it.

('Phrases and Philosophies for the Use of the Young')

The truth is a thing I get rid of as soon as possible... Makes one very unpopular at the club with the older members. They call it being conceited.

(Lord Goring in *An Ideal Husband*)

The truth is rarely pure and never simple. Modern life would be very tedious if it were either, and modern literature a complete impossibility!

(Algernon in *The Importance of Being Earnest*)

REALITY

If one doesn't talk about a thing, it has never happened. It is simply expression… that gives reality to things.

(Dorian in *The Picture of Dorian Gray*)

REASON

I can stand brute force, but brute reason is quite unbearable. There is something unfair about it. It is hitting below the intellect.

(Lord Henry Wotton in *The Picture of Dorian Gray*)

AMBITION

Ambition is the last refuge of the failure.

('Phrases and Philosophies for the Use of the Young')

AND IN CONCLUSION…

Dullness is the coming of age of seriousness.

Nothing that actually occurs is of the smallest importance.

('Phrases and Philosophies for the Use of the Young')

A dreamer is one who can only find his way home by moonlight, and his punishment is that he sees the dawn before the rest of the world.

('The Critic As Artist')

All of the above were, of course, subsumed by that overriding cosmic concept – 'that tiger *Life*' :

> The first duty in life is to be as artificial as possible. What the second duty is no one has yet discovered.
> ('Phrases and Philosophies for the Use of the Young')

> Life… is simply a *mauvais quart d'heure* made up of exquisite moments.
> (Mrs Allonby in *A Woman of No Importance*)

(Interestingly, Andy Warhol was to use precisely that segment of time in his own definition of contemporary fame.)

> Life – coloured turbulent Life – rushes like a river between oneself and those whom one likes, too often.
> (Letter to G. F. Kersley, 1894)

> Life is terribly deficient in form. Its catastrophes happen in the wrong way and to the wrong people. There is a grotesque horror about its comedies, and its tragedies seem to culminate in farce.
> ('The Critic As Artist')

> The secret of life is never to have an emotion that is unbecoming.
> (Mrs Allonby in *A Woman of No Importance*)

I think that life is far too important a thing
ever to talk seriously about it.

(Lord Darlington in *Lady Windermere's Fa*n)

Life is a question of nerves, and fibres, and
slowly built-up cells in which thought hides
and passion has its dreams. You may fancy
yourself safe, and think yourself strong. But
a chance tone of colour in a room or a
morning sky, a particular perfume that you
had once loved and that brings subtle
memories with it, a line from a forgotten
poem that you had come across again, a
cadence from a piece of music that you had
ceased to play… it is on things like this that
our lives depend.

(Lord Henry Wotton in *The Picture of Dorian Gray*)

It is because Humanity has never known
where it was going that it has been able to
find its way.

('The Critic As Artist')

The more one analyses people, the more all
reasons for analysis disappear. Sooner or
later one comes to that dreadful universal
thing called human nature.

('The Decay of Lying')

I hope that you have not exhausted Life...
When a man says that, one knows that Life
has exhausted him.

(Mrs Allonby in *A Woman of No Importance*)

We can have in life one great experience at
best, and the secret of life is to reproduce
that experience as often as possible.

(Lord Henry Wotton in *The Picture of Dorian Gray*)

Try as we may we cannot get behind things
to the reality, and the terrible reason may be
that there is no reality in things apart from
their appearances.

(In conversation)

Later in life, humour goes, but laughter is
the primeval attitude towards life – a mode
of approach that survives only in artists and
criminals.

(Letter to Robert Ross, 1898)

There are few things easier than to live
badly and to die well.

(Prince Paul in *Vera, or The Nihilists*)

By that definition Wilde himself took the more difficult
path.

Certain words and phrases crop up in Wilde's work – probably more often than he realised. 'Nowadays' was one of them, 'an age' another. He was constantly concerned to define the late nineteenth century:

We live in an age where unnecessary things are our only necessities.

(*The Picture of Dorian Gray*)

We live in an age that reads too much to be wise, and thinks too much to be beautiful.

(Lord Henry Wotton in *The Picture of Dorian Gray*)

We are born in an age when only the dull are treated seriously, and I live in terror of being misunderstood.

(Gilbert in 'The Critic As Artist')

We live in the age of the over-worked, and the under-educated; the age in which people are so industrious that they become absolutely stupid.

('The Critic As Artist')

An age with a disgusting appetite for facts.

We live, I regret to say, in an age of surfaces.

(Lady Bracknell in *The Importance of Being Earnest*)

It is a very sad thing that nowadays there is
so little useless information.

('A Few Maxims for the Instruction of the Over-Educated')

He should have lived a century later:

People nowadays are so absolutely
superficial that they don't understand
the philosophy of the superficial.

(Lord Illingworth in *A Woman of No Importance*)

In modern life nothing produces such an
effect as a good platitude. It makes the
whole world kin.

(Mrs Cheveley in *An Ideal Husband*)

We call ourselves a utilitarian age, and we
do not know the uses of any single thing.

(*De Profundis*)

Nowadays people know the price of
everything and the value of nothing.

(Lord Henry Wotton in *The Picture of Dorian Gray*)

What this century worships is wealth. The
God of this century is wealth... At all costs
one must have wealth.

(Sir Robert Chiltern in *An Ideal Husband*)

Nowadays there are so few mysteries left to us that we cannot afford to part with one of them.

('The Critic As Artist')

One can survive anything nowadays except death, and live down anything except a good reputation.

(Lord Illingworth in *A Woman of No Importance*)

In this world there are only two tragedies. One is not getting what one wants and the other is getting it.

(Mr Dumby in *Lady Windermere's Fan*)

Ours is certainly the dullest and most prosaic century possible.

('The Decay of Lying')

Death and vulgarity are the only two facts in the nineteenth century that one cannot explain away.

(Lord Henry Wotton in *The Picture of Dorian Gray*)

The art of living. The only really Fine Art we have produced in modern times.

(Mrs Cheveley in *An Ideal Husband*)

Wilde was to claim that the century had produced only three great personalities – presumably excepting himself – Napoleon, Victor Hugo and Queen Victoria.

How narrow and mean and inadequate to its burdens is this century of ours.

(*De Profundis*)

To realise the nineteenth century, one must realise every century that has preceded it and that has contributed to its making.

WOMEN...
AND MEN

'The Bard of Beauty', 1880

Sphynxes without secrets.
(Lord Henry Wotton defines women in *The Picture of Dorian Gray*)

A misanthrope I can understand – a womanthrope, never.
(Miss Prism in *The Importance of Being Earnest*)

LORD WINDERMERE: How hard good women are!

LADY WINDERMERE: How weak bad men are!
(*Lady Windermere's Fan*)

MRS CHEVELEY: How you men stand up for each other!

LORD GORING: How you women war against each other!
(*An Ideal Husband*)

OSCAR WILDE was very much a ladies' man. Not only did he admire feminine beauty, wit and style when he saw it, he was one of the few in those early pre-feminist days to understand and sympathise with the new role they wished to play in a world about to change irrevocably. In 1887 he took – briefly – his only paid employment. Cassells, the publishers, appointed him as editor of their magazine, *The Lady's World*. One of Wilde's first actions as editor was to insist that it be re-named *The Woman's World*, since he wanted it to be:

> ... the recognised organ for the expression of women's opinions on all subjects of literature and modern life... We should deal not merely with what women wear, but with what they think and what they feel.

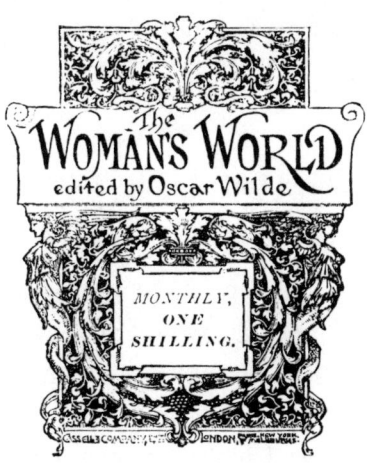

Advertisement for
The Woman's World, *1887*

To a limited degree he was able to put his 'mission statement' into practice, although the chore of office routine
began to cut deeply into his social round and soon had to be
discontinued. However, his tenure, though brief, was bold.
A man who can solicit Gladstone with a verse knows no
boundaries and Wilde even asked Queen Victoria to con-
tribute a poem – only to receive the dusty but distinctly
amused reply: 'Never could the Queen in her whole life
write *one line* of *poetry* serious or comic or make a *Rhyme*
even.' The rejection did nothing to undermine his admiration for his monarch.

'The three women I have most admired are Queen
Victoria, Sarah Bernhardt and Lillie Langtry. I would have
married any one of them with pleasure,' he wrote in 1888.
Whether Her Majesty was amused to find herself in the
company of two actresses is not recorded. Wilde was
always in thrall to the leading actresses of his day. Of
course, he hoped that they would star in the plays he
intended to write (none of them did) but he also admired
them as exquisite examples of their sex.

There was Lillie Langtry (1853–1929):

> ... the adored and adorable Lily...

She was, he said:

> ... a tulip with a figure like a Greek vase
> carved in ivory... I would rather have
> discovered Mrs Langtry than have
> discovered America.

One of the 'Jersey Lily's' more visible roles was that of
sometime mistress to the Prince of Wales (later to be King
Edward VII). Wilde based the character of Mrs Erlynne on

her but when he offered her the part at the age of 39, she asked him how she could possibly play the part of a woman with a grown-up daughter? Perhaps by way of slight reprisal for her refusal, he gave Mrs Erlynne the lines:

> I have never admitted that I am more than twenty-nine or thirty at the most. Twenty-nine when there are pink shades, thirty when there are not.
>
> (*Lady Windermere's Fan*)

He also paid court to the French actress, Sarah Bernhardt (1844–1923) in the hope that she would play the lead in his *Salomé*. She was, he felt, like 'the serpent of the old Nile, older than the Pyramids' and he composed a poem in her honour:

> *Ah, surely once some urn of Attic clay*
> *Held thy wan dust, and thou has come again*
> *Back to this common world so dull and vain.*

For Ellen Terry (1847–1928), England's pre-eminent actress of the day, he wrote:

> *She stands with eyes marred by the mists*
> *of pain*
> *Like some wan lily overdrenched with*
> *rain...*
> *O Hair of Gold! O Crimson Lips! O Face*
> *Made for the luring and the love of man!*

Perhaps it was the overblown verse that was the deciding factor.

Heroine worship aside, in his mature work Wilde was able to skewer the social attitudes that divided the Victorian sexes and demonstrate their essential interdependence. Each of the plays has a character to express the male chauvinist point of view and an articulate woman (or two) to underline the fact that a man does what a woman decides to *let* him decide to do. He depicts it as a complex dance with all the movements carefully orchestrated. First, though, one must define the points of similarity and difference between women and men:

LORD ILLINGWORTH: The Book of Life begins with a man and a woman in a garden.

MRS ALLONBY: It ends with Revelations.

(*A Woman of No Importance*)

Men can be analysed, women… merely adored.

(Mrs Cheveley in *An Ideal Husband*)

Women are pictures. Men are problems.

Women are meant to be loved, not to be understood.

(Lord Illingworth in *A Woman of No Importance*)

LORD ILLINGWORTH: We men know life too early.

MRS ALLONBY: And we women know life
too late. That is the difference between
men and women.

(*A Woman of No Importance*)

Women are never disarmed by compliments.
Men always are. That is the difference
between the sexes.

(Mrs Cheveley in *An Ideal Husband*)

My dear young lady, there was a great deal
of truth, I dare say, in what you said, and
you looked very pretty while you said it,
which is much more important.

(Lady Hunstanton in *A Woman of No Importance*)

[Women] have always been picturesque
protests against the mere existence of
common sense. We saw its dangers from
the first.

(Mrs Allonby in *A Woman of No Importance*)

LORD ILLINGWORTH: All women become
like their mothers. That is their Tragedy.
MRS ALLONBY: No man does. That is his.

(*A Woman of No Importance*)

Between men and women there is no friendship possible. There is passion, enmity, worship, love, but no friendship.

(Lord Darlington in *Lady Windermere's Fan*)

How absurd to talk of the equality of the sexes! Where questions of self-sacrifice are concerned, men are infinitely beyond us.

(Gwendolen in *The Importance of Being Earnest*)

A man who moralises is usually a hypocrite, and a woman who moralises is invariably plain.

(Mr Cecil Graham in *Lady Windermere's Fan*)

Plain women are always jealous of their husbands, beautiful women never are!

(Mrs Allonby in *A Woman of No Importance*)

A man's face is his autobiography. A woman's is her work of fiction.

(To Robert Ross)

LADY STUTFIELD: Ah! The world was made for men and not for women.

MRS ALLONBY: We have a much better time than they do. There are far more

things forbidden to us than there are
to them.

(*A Woman of No Importance*)

Mrs Allonby becomes the 'spokesperson' – as we would
now carefully call it – for her sex in this, Wilde's second
major play:

The annoying thing is that the wretches can
be perfectly happy without us. That is why I
think it is every woman's duty never to leave
them alone for a single moment... They are
horribly tedious when they are good
husbands, and abominably conceited when
they are not... My husband is a sort of
promissory note: I'm tired of meeting him...
We women adore failures. They lean on us...
We are the laurels to hide their baldness...
Nothing is so aggravating as calmness.
There is something positively brutal about
the good temper of most modern men. I
wonder that we women stand it as well as
we do... How can a woman expect to be
happy with a man who insists on treating
her as if she were a perfectly rational
being?... All men are married women's
property. That is the only true definition of
what married women's property really is.

The Ideal Man should talk to us as if we

were goddesses, and treat us as if we were children... He should invariably praise us for whatever qualities he knows we haven't got. But he should be pitiless in reproaching us for the virtues that we never dreamed of possessing.

The Ideal Man... should always say much more than he means, and always mean much more than he says... He should never run down pretty women. That would show he had no taste or make one suspect that he had too much. No, he should be nice about them all, don't say that somehow they don't attract him.

Her principal sparring partner in the play is Lord Illingworth, whose views (summarised here) are invariably a mirror image of her own:

Women love us for our defects. If we have enough of them, they will forgive us anything, even our giant intellects... You women live by your emotions and for them. You have no philosophy of life... Women should think in moderation, as they should do all things in moderation... You should never try to understand them... If you want to know what a woman really means – which, by the way, is always a dangerous thing to do – look at her,

don't listen to her... Women forgive adoration; that is quite as much as should be
expected from them... I don't mind plain
women being Puritans. It is the only excuse
they have for being plain... What a typical
woman you are! You talk sentimentally and
you are thoroughly selfish the whole time.

His brother-in-chauvinist-arms is Lord Henry Wotton in
The Picture of Dorian Gray:

The only way a woman can reform a man
is by boring him so completely that he loses
all interest in life... Women appreciate
cruelty... They have wonderfully primitive
instincts. We have emancipated them, but
they remain slaves looking for their masters,
all the same. They love being dominated...
They flaunt their conjugal felicity in one's
face, as if it were the most fascinating of
sins... Women represent the triumph of
matter over mind – just as men represent the
triumph of mind over morals... The history
of women is the history of the worst form of
tyranny the world has ever known. The
tyranny of the weak over the strong...
Women are a fascinatingly wilful sex. Every
woman is a rebel, and usually in wild revolt
against herself.

Women, as some witty Frenchman once put it, inspire us with the desire to do masterpieces, and always prevent us from carrying them out.

(Lord Henry Wotton in *The Picture of Dorian Gray*)

Men become old, but they never become good.

(Duchess of Berwick in *Lady Windermere's Fan*)

In fact, some men are simply beyond female redemption:

He has one of those terribly weak natures that are not susceptible to influence.

(Mabel Chiltern in *An Ideal Husband*)

I don't think man has much capacity for development. He has got as far as he can, and that is not far, is it?

(Lady Markby in *An Ideal Husband*)

Not surprisingly, the male point of view was a little different:

I like men who have a future and women who have a past.

(Lord Henry Wotton in *The Picture of Dorian Gray*)

The true perfection of man lies, not in what man has, but in what man is.

('The Soul of Man Under Socialism')

[*146*]

A point that was hardly lost on their womenfolk:

> Many a woman has a past, but I am told that
> she has at least a dozen, and that they all fit.
> (Duchess of Berwick of Mrs Erlynne in *Lady Windermere's Fan*)

> There is a fashion in pasts just as there is a
> fashion in frocks. Perhaps Mrs Cheveley's
> past is merely a slightly *décolletée* one, and
> they are excessively popular nowadays.
> (Lord Goring in *An Ideal Husband*)

> She is without one good quality... I haven't
> a word to say in her favour... and she is one
> of my greatest friends.
> (In conversation)

> Women of that kind are most useful. They
> form the basis of other people's marriages.
> (Lady Plymdale in *Lady Windermere's Fan*)

Mrs Allonby was in no doubt about the definition of a 'bad woman':

> ... the sort of woman a man never gets tired
> of...

> If a woman wants to hold a man, she has
> merely to appeal to the worst in him.
> (Lady Windermere in *Lady Windermere's Fan*)

But perhaps Lord Illingworth is the character most likely to raise feminist hackles today:

> I don't think there is a woman in the world who would not be a little flattered if one made love to her. It is that which makes women so irresistibly adorable.

Although Lord Henry and Lord Goring are runners-up:

> DORIAN: You must admit that women give to men the very gold of their lives.
> LORD HENRY WOTTON: Possibly, but they invariably want it back in such very small change.
> (*The Picture of Dorian Gray*)

> A man's life is of more value than a woman's. It has larger issues, wider scope, greater ambitions. A woman's life revolves in curves of emotions.
> (Lord Goring in *An Ideal Husband*)

When he was not helping his characters to fight the undeclared battle of the sexes, Wilde took the time to speculate on the essential qualities of Woman:

> ALGERNON: I thought every woman had a mission of some kind, nowadays.
> CECILY: Every female has! No woman.
> (*The Importance of Being Earnest*)

If a woman can't make her mistakes
charming, she is only a female.
(Lord Arthur Savile in 'Lord Arthur Savile's Crime')

SIR ROBERT CHILTERN: You think
science cannot grapple with the problem
of women?
MRS CHEVELEY: Science can never
grapple with the irrational.
SIR ROBERT CHILTERN: And women
represent the irrational.
MRS CHEVELEY: Well-dressed women do.
(*An Ideal Husband*)

I don't know that women are always
rewarded for being charming. I think they
are usually punished for it.
(Mrs Cheveley in *An Ideal Husband*)

Many other female qualities had an element of paradox
about them, according to Wilde:

Why, she is worse than ugly, she is good.
(*The Duchess of Padua*)

She is better than good – she is beautiful. It
is better to be beautiful than to be good
but... it is better to be good than to be ugly.
(Lord Henry Wotton in *The Picture of Dorian Gray*)

It takes a thoroughly good woman to do a thoroughly stupid thing.

(Lady Plymdale in *Lady Windermere's Fan*)

Wicked women bother one. Good women bore one. That is the only difference between them.

(Mr Cecil Graham in *Lady Windermere's Fan*)

Women have no appreciation of good looks; at least, good women have not.

(Lord Henry Wotton in *The Picture of Dorian Gray*)

Ordinary women never appeal to one's imagination. They are limited to their century... No glamour ever transfigures them. One knows their minds as easily as one knows their bonnets.

(Dorian in *The Picture of Dorian Gray*)

Memory, it seemed, was a quality best forgotten:

No woman should have a memory. Memory in a woman is the beginning of dowdiness.

(Lord Illingworth in *A Woman of No Importance*)

Women are the most reliable, as they have no memory for the important.

(Letter to Ross from Reading prison)

Good memories are not a quality that
women admire much in men.

(Cecily in *The Importance of Being Earnest*)

Then there was the question of woman's intuition:

Women have a wonderful instinct about
things. They can discover everything except
the obvious.

(Lord Goring in *An Ideal Husband*)

And one incontrovertible truth:

Every woman does talk too much.

(Colonel Kotemkin in *Vera, or The Nihilists*)

There is only one real tragedy in a woman's
life. The fact that her past is always her
lover, and her future invariably her
husband.

(Mrs Cheveley in *An Ideal Husband*)

Perhaps the bleakest verdict came from Lord Henry:

Women never know when the curtain has
fallen. They always want a sixth act... If
they were allowed their own way, every
comedy would have a tragic ending, and
every tragedy would culminate in a farce.

Wilde considered himself an authority on all matters that involved taste. The small matter of how a woman should *dress* was one he took in his stride. He advised them to give up bustles and corsets. The focus of clothing should be the shoulders, not the waist and it should favour the draped, classical Greek look. High heels were to be avoided. They put a strain on the body and threw a woman forward. And as for artificial flowers... The work is littered with asides on feminine appearance. Mrs Cheveley, for instance, is introduced in a stage direction as looking:

> ... rather like an orchid... a work of art on the whole, but showing the influence of too many schools.

In *The Picture of Dorian Gray*, Lady Narborough, who has 'the remains of really remarkable ugliness', insisted on going *décolletée* and looked 'like an *édition de luxe* of a bad French novel'. When her third husband died, 'her hair turned quite gold from grief'. The Duchess of Harley possessed:

> ... those ample architectural proportions that in women who are not Duchesses are described by contemporary historians as stoutness...

Mrs Vandeleur, though 'a perfect saint among women', was:

> ... so dreadfully dowdy that she reminded one of a badly bound hymn book...

Lady Brandon was 'a peacock in everything but beauty', while Lord Henry's wife, Victoria, is described as:

... a curious woman, whose dresses always looked as if they had been designed in a rage and put on in a tempest... She tried to look picturesque but only succeeded in looking untidy.

She left the room:

... looking like a bird of paradise that had been out all night in the rain, leaving a faint odour of frangipani...

Lord Henry's rule of thumb was to:

Never trust a woman who wears mauve, whatever her age may be, or a woman over thirty-five who is fond of pink ribbons. It always means that they have a history.

A woman whose size in gloves is seven and three-quarters never knows much about anything.
(Mrs Cheveley in *An Ideal Husband*)

She wore far too much rouge last night, and not quite enough clothes. That is always a sign of despair in a woman.
(Lord Goring in *An Ideal Husband*)

If a woman really repents, she has to go to a bad dressmaker, otherwise no one believes in her.

(Mrs Erlynne in *Lady Windermere's Fan*)

She was simply perfectly proportioned – a rare thing in an age when so many women are either over life-size or insignificant.

(Said of Sybil Merton in 'Lord Arthur Savile's Crime')

I think men are the only authorities on dress.

(Mrs Cheveley in *An Ideal Husband*)

It would be nice to think that it was his desire to pursue the 'perfect proportions' that led Wilde to lend his name to an advertisement for Madame Fontaine's Bosom Beautifier, the copy for which – presumably *not* by Wilde! – read:

Just as sure as the sun will rise tomorrow, just so sure will it enlarge and beautify the bosom.

And finally – Wilde on How A Woman Should Behave:

Crying is the refuge of plain women but the ruin of pretty ones.

(Duchess of Berwick in *Lady Windermere's Fan*)

One should never trust a woman who tells
one her real age. A woman who would tell
one that, would tell one anything.

(Lord Illingworth in *A Woman of No Importance*)

No woman should ever be quite accurate
about her age. It looks so calculating...
Thirty-five is a very attractive age. London
Society is full of women of the very highest
birth who have, of their own free choice,
remained thirty-five for years.

(Lady Bracknell in *The Importance of Being Earnest*)

Nowadays it is not fashionable to flirt till
one is forty, or to be romantic till one is forty-
five, so we poor women who are under
thirty, or say we are, have nothing open to us
but politics or philanthropy.

(Mrs Cheveley in *An Ideal Husband*)

[High intellectual pressure] is the most
unbecoming thing there is. It makes the
noses of the young girls so particularly large.
And there is nothing so difficult to marry as
a large nose; men don't like them.

(Lady Markby in *An Ideal Husband*)

Advertisement for
'Madame Fontaine's Beauty Cream',
1882

As long as a woman can look ten years younger than her own daughter, she is perfectly satisfied.

(Lord Henry Wotton in *The Picture of Dorian Gray*)

LOVE AND
MARRIAGE
...AND SEX

*Oscar as seen by a fellow
undergraduate, 1881*

What a silly thing love is! It is not half as useful as logic, for it does not prove anything and it is always telling one things that are not going to happen, and making one believe things that are not true.

('The Nightingale and the Rose')

When you really want love, you will find it waiting for you.

(*De Profundis*)

BASIL HALLWARD: Love is a more wonderful thing than art.

LORD HENRY: They are both simply forms of imitation.

(*The Picture of Dorian Gray*)

IN THAT NO MAN'S LAND where the sexes skirmish, the eternal game is Romance and all the players have to find out the rules for themselves:

> I am not at all romantic. I am not old enough. I leave romance to my seniors.
>
> (Lord Goring in *An Ideal Husband*)

> Each time one loves is the only time one has ever loved... The people who only love once in their lives are the shallow people.
>
> (Lord Henry Wotton in *The Picture of Dorian Gray*)

> The very essence of romance is uncertainty.
>
> (Algernon in *The Importance of Being Earnest*)

> Women... spoil every romance by trying to make it last for ever... The only difference between a caprice and a life-long passion is that the caprice lasts a little longer... The worst of having a romance of any kind is that it leaves one so unromantic.
>
> (Lord Henry Wotton in *The Picture of Dorian Gray*)

> When one is in love one begins by deceiving oneself, and one ends by deceiving others. That is what the world calls a romance... Nothing spoils a romance so much as a sense

of humour in a woman.

(Lord Illingworth in *A Woman of No Importance*)

To which Mrs Allonby replied: 'Or the want of it in a man.'

There is no such thing as a romantic experience; there are romantic memories, and
there is the desire for romance – that is all.

(1886)

There was the 'female of the species':

The only way to behave to a woman is to
make love to her, if she is pretty, and to
someone else, if she is plain.

(Algernon in *The Importance of Being Earnest*)

But then the creatures are not to be trusted:

[Good looks] are a snare that every sensible
man would like to be caught in.

(Algernon in *The Importance of Being Earnest*)

A woman will flirt with anybody in the
world as long as other people are looking on.

(Lord Henry Wotton in *The Picture of Dorian Gray*)

Girls never marry the men they flirt with.
Girls don't think it right.

(Algernon in *The Importance of Being Earnest*)

She'll never love you unless you are at her
heels; women like to be bothered.

(Peter in *Vera, or the Nihilists*)

In the case of very fascinating women, sex is
a challenge, not a defence.

(Lord Goring in *An Ideal Husband*)

Man is constant in his infidelity and woman
puts him to shame because she is, by nature,
fickle.

(In conversation)

Not too surprisingly, women saw things from a rather different point of view:

We women love with our ears, just as you men
love with your eyes, if you ever love at all.

(Duchess of Monmouth in *The Picture of Dorian Gray*)

But love, romance, passion – whatever you choose to call it
and should it exist – was by no means for everyone:

Romance is the privilege of the rich, not the
profession of the unemployed.

('The Model Millionaire')

A *grande passion*... is the privilege of people
who have nothing to do. That is one use of
the idle classes of a country... Nothing is

serious except passion. The Intellect is not a
serious thing, and never has been. It is an
instrument on which one plays, that is all.

(Lord Illingworth in *A Woman of No Importance*)

The female perspective on the whole business invariably
turns out to be the more 'realistic':

Men always want to be a woman's first
love… What we like is to be a man's last
romance… He swore to me positively on his
knees that he had never loved anyone before
in the whole course of his life… I found out
that what he had said was perfectly true.
And that sort of thing makes a man so
absolutely uninteresting.

(Mrs Allonby in *A Woman of No Importance*)

More women grow old nowadays through
the faithfulness of their admirers than
through anything else! At least that is the
only way I can account for the terribly
haggard look of most of your pretty women
in London!

(Mrs Cheveley in *An Ideal Husband*)

I delight in men over seventy. They bring
one the devotion of a lifetime.

(Mrs Allonby in *A Woman of No Importance*)

Love, after all – like reputation – is merely a bubble...

> Love is easily killed. Oh, how easily love is killed.
>
> (Mrs Erlynne in *Lady Windermere's Fan*)

> One should always be in love. That is the reason one should never marry.
>
> (Lord Henry Wotton in *The Picture of Dorian Gray*)

> A kiss may ruin a human life.
>
> (Mrs Arbuthnot in *A Woman of No Importance*)

> Treachery is inseparable from faith. I often betray myself with a kiss.
>
> (To Ada Leverson, 1894)

> I suppose that when a man has once loved a woman, he will do anything for her, except continue to love her?
>
> (Mrs Cheveley in *An Ideal Husband*)

So how does one end it?

> All romances should end in a sonnet. I suppose all romances do.
>
> (Letter to Reggie Turner, 1898)

There is always something ridiculous about the emotions of people whom one has ceased to love.

(Lord Henry Wotton in *The Picture of Dorian Gray*)

But by the end Wilde came to a more philosophical point of view. Or perhaps he was simply paring the subject down to its core:

And so from youth to manhood do we go,
And fall to weary days and locks of snow.
Love only knows no winter; never dies.

(*Ravenna*)

For most of Wilde's characters and for most of Victorian society, Love had only one desirable outcome – particularly for the mothers:

Not love at first sight, but love at the end of the season, which is so much more satisfactory.

(Duchess of Berwick in *Lady Windermere's Fan*)

An engagement should come on a young girl as a surprise, pleasant or unpleasant, as the case may be... I am not in favour of long engagements. They give people the opportunity of finding out each other's character before marriage, which I think is never advisable.

(Lady Bracknell in *The Importance of Being Earnest*)

Once a week is quite enough to propose to anyone, and it should always be done in a manner that attracts some attention.

(Mabel Chiltern in *An Ideal Husband*)

It is said, of course, that she ran away twice before she was married. But you know how unfair people often are. I myself don't believe she ran away more than once.

(Lady Caroline in *A Woman of No Importance*)

To elope is cowardly. It's running away from danger. And danger has become so rare in modern life.

(Mrs Allonby in *A Woman of No Importance*)

There was that endangered species, the Bachelor:

Rich bachelors should be heavily taxed. It is not fair that some men should be happier than others.

(In conversation)

By remaining persistently single, a man converts himself into a permanent public temptation. Men should be more careful; their very celibacy leads weaker vessels astray.

(Miss Prism in *The Importance of Being Earnest*)

Damme, sir, it is your duty to get married.
You can't always be living for pleasure.
Every man of position is married nowadays.
Bachelors are not fashionable any more.
They are a damaged lot. Too much is known
about them. You must get a wife, sir!

(Lord Caversham in *An Ideal Husband*)

If we men married the women we deserved,
we should have a very bad time of it... It is
the growth of the moral sense of women that
makes marriage such a hopeless, one-sided
institution.

(Lord Goring in *An Ideal Husband*)

Women are wonderfully practical... In
situations of that kind we often forget to say
anything about marriage and they always
remind us.

(Lord Henry Wotton in *The Picture of Dorian Gray*)

I have always been of the opinion that a man
who desires to get married should know
either everything or nothing.

(Lady Bracknell in *The Importance of Being Earnest*)

And so they were married and lived... ?

The proper basis for marriage is a mutual misunderstanding.

(Lord Arthur in 'Lord Arthur Savile's Crime')

The very essence of marriage is uncertainty. If ever I get married, I'll certainly try to forget the fact.

(Algernon in *The Importance of Being Earnest*)

The real drawback to marriage is that it makes one unselfish. And unselfish people are colourless... The one charm of marriage is that it makes a life of deception absolutely necessary for both parties... Men marry because they are tired; women because they are curious. Both are disappointed... the happiness of a married man... depends on the people he has not married.

(Lord Henry Wotton in *The Picture of Dorian Gray*)

How marriage ruins a man. It's as demoralising as cigarettes, and far more expensive.

(Mr Dumby in *Lady Windermere's Fan*)

The game of marriage... the wives hold all the honours, and invariably lose the odd trick.

(Lord Darlington in *Lady Windermere's Fan*)

To which the Duchess of Berwick replies:

> The odd trick? Is that the husband, Lord
> Darlington?

There was Getting Married... and then there was the *State*
of Marriage:

> As for domesticity, it ages one rapidly, and
> distracts one's mind from higher things.
> (The Rocket in 'The Remarkable Rocket')

> I have often observed that in married
> households the champagne is rarely of a
> first-rate vintage.
> (Lane, the Butler in *The Importance of Being Earnest*)

> For an artist to marry his model is as fatal as
> for a gourmet to marry his cook; the one gets
> no sittings and the other gets no dinners.
> ('London Models')

> The husbands of very beautiful women
> belong to the criminal classes.
> (Lord Henry Wotton in *The Picture of Dorian Gray*)

> [My husband] is the general rule, and
> nothing ages a woman so rapidly as having
> married the general rule.
> (Lady Markby in *An Ideal Husband*)

The amount of women in London who flirt with their own husbands is perfectly scandalous. It looks so bad. It is like washing one's clean linen in public.

(Algernon in *The Importance of Being Earnest*)

✒

It's most dangerous for a husband to pay attention to his wife in public. It always makes people think that he beats her when they're alone.

(Lady Plymdale in *Lady Windermere's Fan*)

✒

ALGERNON: You don't seem to realise that in married life three is company and two is none.

JACK: That is the theory that the corrupt French drama has been propounding for the last fifty years.

(*The Importance of Being Earnest*)

✒

MRS CHEVELEY: What do you know about my married life?

LORD GORING: Nothing; but I can read it like a book.

MRS CHEVELEY: What book?

LORD GORING: The Book of Numbers.

(*An Ideal Husband*)

[*169*]

Nowadays all married men live like bachelors, and all the bachelors like married men.
(Lady Narborough in *The Picture of Dorian Gray*)

I hope marriage has not made you too
serious? It has never had that effect on me.
(To Charles Mason, one of the 'rent' boys, 1894)

No married man is ever attractive except to
his wife.
(Miss Prism in *The Importance of Being Earnest*)

There's nothing in the world like the devotion of a married woman. It's a thing no
married man knows anything about.
(Mr Cecil Graham in *Lady Windermere's Fan*)

London is full of women who trust their
husbands. One can always recognise them.
They look thoroughly unhappy.
(Lady Windermere in *Lady Windermere's Fan*)

He was dreadfully short-sighted, and there
is no pleasure in taking a husband who
never sees anything.
(Lady Narborough in *The Picture of Dorian Gray*)

When a woman finds out about her
husband, she either becomes dreadfully
dowdy, or wears very smart bonnets that
some other woman's husband has to pay for.
(Lord Henry Wotton in *The Picture of Dorian Gray*)

Young men want to be faithful, and are not;
old men want to be faithless, and cannot.
(Lord Henry Wotton in *The Picture of Dorian Gray*)

Then time takes its toll...

Twenty years of romance makes a woman
look like a ruin; but twenty years of
marriage makes her something like a public
building.
(Lord Illingworth in *A Woman of No Importance*)

When a woman marries again it is because
she detested her first husband. When a man
marries again, it is because he adored his
first wife. Women try their luck; men risk
theirs... What nonsense people talk about
happy marriages! A man can be happy with
any woman, as long as he does not love her.
(Lord Henry Wotton in *The Picture of Dorian Gray*)

Wilde was to say at the time (1890) that:

Lord Henry's views on marriage are quite

monstrous and I highly disapprove of them.
(Letter to Arthur Fish)

Nothing should surprise us nowadays,
except happy marriages.
(Lady Caroline in *A Woman of No Importance*)

Let me see – you have been married twice
already; suppose you try falling in love for
once.
(Prince Paul in *Vera, or The Nihilists*)

She has more than once changed her
husband… but as she had never changed her
lover, the world had long ago ceased to talk
scandal about her.
(Said of Lady Windermere in 'Lord Arthur Savile's Crime')

Nowadays people marry as often as they
can, don't they? It is most fashionable.
(Lady Markby in *An Ideal Husband*)

In married life affection comes when people
thoroughly dislike each other.
(Lord Goring in *An Ideal Husband*)

Divorces were made in heaven.

(Algernon in *The Importance of Being Earnest*)

But perhaps, after all, the more considered view was more benevolent and more typically Wilde:

The bond of all companionship, whether in marriage or in friendship, is conversation.

(*De Profundis*)

As a young man, Wilde was often in love and, in 1875, while still a student, was unofficially 'engaged' to Florence Balcombe. Neither had any money and events soon parted them but he never forgot her. In May 1884, he married the rather more moneyed Constance Lloyd. He wrote to a friend, American sculptor, Waldo Story:

She is quite young, very grave, and mystical, with wonderful eyes, and dark brown coils of hair... We are, of course, desperately in love... we telegraph to each other twice a day, and the telegraph clerks have become quite romantic in consequence. I hand in my messages, however, very sternly, and try to look as if 'love' was a cryptogram for 'Buy Grand Trunks', and 'darling' a cypher for 'sell out at par'. I am sure it succeeds... She knows I am the greatest poet, so in literature she is all right.

Constance Wilde, 1892

> She never speaks and I am always
> wondering what her thoughts are like...
> (In conversation)

There were two sons born just over a year apart:

> [The baby] has a superb voice, which it freely
> exercises: its style is essentially Wagnerian.

But much as Wilde loved them both:

> Desire is killed by maternity; passion buried
> in conception.

He told Frank Harris:

> When I married, my wife was a beautiful
> girl, white and slim as a lily with dancing
> eyes and gay rippling laughter like music.
> In a year or so all the flowerlike grace had
> vanished; she became heavy, shapeless,
> deformed.

He had to force himself...

> ... to touch and kiss her... I used to wash my
> mouth and open the window to cleanse my
> lips in the pure air.

They were to remain married until her death in 1898, although estranged after his prison sentence. He never saw his sons again. Perhaps a prescient summation of the relationship came from Sir Robert Chiltern in *An Ideal Husband* (1895):

Loveless marriages are horrible. But there is one thing worse... a marriage in which there is love, but on one side only; faith, but on one side only; devotion, but on one side only and in which of the two hearts one is sure to be broken.

Constance and Cyril Wilde, c.1894

And then there was – Sex, something which more common-
ly appeared under one of its various pseudonyms. With the
unquestionable wisdom of hindsight and a pinch of psychi-
atric jargon it is easy to conclude that Wilde was always a
latent homosexual who took the trouble to cover his tracks
for much of his adult life. Certainly there was 'Wasted
Days', the 1877 sonnet to a young boy that spoke of:

> *A fair slim boy made not for this world's*
> *pain,*
> *With hair of gold thick clustering round*
> *his ears...*
> *Pale cheeks whereon no kiss hath left its*
> *stain,*
> *Red under-lip drawn in for fear of love,*
> *And white throat whiter than the breast of*
> *dove...*

By the time it appeared in the collected *Poems* (1881) the
boy had become a 'lily-girl' with 'brown soft hair close
braided by her ears' and the sonnet was now called
'Madonna Mia'.

The fact remains that, in his school days, Wilde recalled:

No one appeared to care for sex. We were
healthy young barbarians and that was all.

The idea of 'Greek love' began to appeal in his Oxford
days, along with the whole intellectual concept of Hellenic
life.

Even in court he could defend it articulately:

The 'Love that dare not speak its name' [*a*
phrase coined by Douglas in a poem] in this

century is such a great affection of an elder
for a younger man as there was between
David and Jonathan, such as Plato made the
very basis of his philosophy, and such as you
find in the sonnets of Michaelangelo and
Shakespeare... It is that deep, spiritual affection that is as pure as it is perfect... It is in
this century misunderstood, so much misunderstood that it may be described as the
'Love that dare not speak its name' and on
account of it I am placed where I am now. It
is beautiful, it is fine, it is the noblest form of
affection. There is nothing unnatural about
it. It is intellectual and it frequently exists
between an elder and a younger man, when
the elder man has intellect, and the younger
man has all the joy, hope and glamour of life
before him. That it should be so the world
does not understand. The world mocks at it
and sometimes puts one in the pillory for it.

In saying it, however, Wilde was being personally disingen-
uous – not to say dishonest. Whatever he may have believed
intellectually, by this time (1895) he was a practising homosexual, having – by his own admission – been seduced by
Robert Ross in 1886. The next several years were, by all
accounts, an agonising personal struggle as he tried to
define his true nature.

Then, in early 1891 he met Lord Alfred Douglas ('Bosie'),
younger son of the Marquis of Queensberry, and the balance

was irrevocably tipped. By 1892 he can describe Bosie as 'quite like a narcissus – so white and gold... he lies like a hyacinth on the sofa and I worship him'.

Constance was a 'lily' but Bosie a 'narcissus' or 'hyacinth'. Flowers were the language of Love for Wilde, portents of both pleasure and Destruction:

> There is an unknown land full of strange flowers and subtle perfumes, a land of which it is joy of all joys to dream, a land where all things are perfect and poisonous.
>
> (Letter to Harry Marillier, 1884)

> Even the scarlet flowers of passion seem to grow in the same meadow as the poppies of oblivion.
>
> (Erskine in *The Portrait of Mr W. H.*, 1889)

Prison left him without any real hope of redemption. The last years were a descending spiral, sexually and in every other way.

He was to have one more half-hearted attempt at hetero-sexuality when he was persuaded to visit a brothel in Dieppe with Ernest Dowson. He recalled the experience as like 'chewing cold mutton. But tell it in England, where it will entirely restore my reputation.'

> How evil it is to buy Love, and how evil to sell it! And yet what purple hours one can snatch from that grey slow-moving thing we call time!
>
> (Letter to Robert Ross, May 1900)

In *De Profundis* he had, for the moment, travelled hopeful-
ly when he wrote:

> When you really want love, you will find it
> waiting for you.

In his own case it was to be an appointment that was not
kept.

THE 'PROFESSOR OF AESTHETICS AND CRITIC OF ART'

'Happy as a Bright Sunflower', 1881

The secret of Life is art.

(US lecture tour)

All art is quite useless.

(Preface to *The Picture of Dorian Gray* – a concept he had 'borrowed' from Gautier and Whistler, meaning that Art should not be used for political, religious or social purposes)

I look forward to the time when aesthetics will take the place of ethics, when the sense of beauty will be the dominant law of life: It will never be so, and so I look forward to it.

(Letter to Mrs Lathbury, 1890)

If one loves Art at all, one must love it beyond all other things in the world.

('The Critic As Artist')

IN HIS EARLY ATTEMPTS to be either famous or notorious, Wilde succeeded in being both by the extreme views he expressed on 'Art'. They were calculated to infuriate almost everyone by the iconoclastic and paradoxical way he chose to express them and reading them today it is clear that the tongue was often firmly in the Wilde cheek.

So much of a caricature did he appear in that early post-Oxford phase that he was a natural target for the satire of magazines like *Punch*, where George du Maurier consistently lampooned him as Oscuro Wildgoose, Drawit Wilde, the Wilde-eyed poet and Ossian Wilderness.

He was a sufficiently mainstream figure to attract the attention of Gilbert and Sullivan in their 1881 *Patience*, although they were careful to make it clear that theirs was not an attack on the whole aesthetic movement but merely on 'the unmanly oddities which masquerade in its likeness.'

Before he moved into his 'second phase', Wilde reflected on how so little actual achievement had resulted in so large a return in terms of celebrity:

> To have done it was nothing but to make
> people *think* one had done it was a triumph.

Not that his underlying beliefs, drawn from Ruskin and Pater – and, earlier still, the Pre-Raphaelites – were not sincerely held. In later years he simply toned down the expression of them somewhat. By that time, however, much of the damage was done in the eyes of his critics. He may have considered himself a 'Professor of Aesthetics' but many of them thought him 'The High Priest of the Decadents' (*National Observer*).

The Gospel According to Wilde was what he termed the 'New Hedonism'. In its extreme form its philosophy was defined by Lord Henry Wotton in *The Picture of Dorian Gray* as a movement...

> ... that was to recreate life and to save it from that harsh, uncomely puritanism that is having, in our own day, a curious revival. It was to have its service of intellect, certainly; yet it was never to accept any theory or system that would involve the sacrifice of any mode of passionate experience.

And elsewhere:

> ... a fresh school that is to have in it all the passion of the romantic spirit, all the passion of the spirit that is Greek... The new Hellenism, in which the best of Greek culture and Christian culture can be synthesized.

Art in its broadest sense – Wilde believed – was the medium that could realise and release the New Hellenism. In saying so to a society of primly realistic Victorians who only trusted in what they could touch or measure, he was chipping away at the bedrock of their beliefs. By the *agent provocateur* expression of his views, moreover, he was doing precisely the same thing to his own ultimate security.

What did the fellow mean by saying that: 'The telling of beautiful untrue things is the proper aim of Art'? Or: 'A truth in Art is one whose contrary is equally true'? And why did the word always have to have a capital 'A'?

The aphorisms never stopped flowing – even when Wilde 2 was created. If anything, the reaction to his paradoxes spurred him to fresh heights, as in the 1889 essay, 'The Decay of Lying':

'A Thing of Beauty Not a Joy Forever', 1883

The object of Art is not simple truth but complex beauty.

The proper school to learn art is not Life but Art.

As long as a thing is useful or necessary to us... it is outside the proper sphere of Art.

Art never expresses anything but itself.

He then recalled:

that hackneyed passage [*in Shakespeare*] about Art holding the mirror up to Nature,

[*185*]

forgetting that this unfortunate aphorism is deliberately said by Hamlet in order to convince the bystanders of his absolute insanity on all art-matters.

('The Decay of Lying')

For had he not already decreed that:

It is the spectator, and not life, that Art really mirrors.

(Preface to *The Picture of Dorian Gray*)

And the 1891 'The Soul Of Man Under Socialism':

Art is the most intense mode of Individualism that the world has known.

But the verbal time bomb was buried in such remarks as:

The sphere of Art and the sphere of ethics are absolutely distinct and separate.

(Reply to a critic)

Wilde believed passionately that there was and should be a clear division between Art and Life.

What is abnormal in Life stands in normal relation to Art. It is the only thing in Life that stands in normal relation to Art.

('A Few Maxims for the Instruction of the Over-Educated')

The impossible in Art is anything that has
happened in real life.

The realistic school of art held little attraction for him –
when viewing Frith's monumental canvas, 'Derby Day', he
is supposed to have remarked: 'Is it really ALL done by
hand? – nor did the art establishment:

Varnishing is the only artistic process
with which the Royal Academicians
are thoroughly familiar.

On a staircase stood several Royal
Academicians, disguised as artists.

(In conversation)

There are two ways of disliking art... One is
to dislike it. The other, to like it rationally...
it is only an auctioneer who can equally and
impartially admire all schools of art... The
best that one can say of most modern
creative art is that it is just a little less vulgar
than reality.

('The Critic As Artist')

All archaeological pictures that make you
say, 'How curious'; all sentimental pictures
that make you say, 'How sad'; all historical

pictures that make you say, 'How interesting'; all pictures that do not immediately
give you such artistic joy as to make you say,
'How beautiful', are bad pictures.

('Lecture to Art Students')

He professed to believe that Art was not simply a way to
express and interpret aspects of the world around us. It was
quite the other way round:

Life imitates Art far more than Art imitates
Life… a great artist invents a type and life
tries to copy it… Life is Art's best, Art's only
pupil.

Art takes Life as part of her rough material,
recreates it, and refashions it in fresh forms,
is absolutely indifferent to fact, invents,
imagines, dreams and keeps between herself
and reality the impenetrable barrier of
beautiful style, of decorative or ideal
treatment.

(*The Picture of Dorian Gray*)

Art is our spirited protest, our gallant
attempt to teach Nature her proper place.

('The Decay of Lying')

This sentiment provides the elusive explanation for the origin of 'that magnificent flower', the famous dyed 'green
carnation', first worn by Robert Ross at the opening night

of *Lady Windermere's Fan* in 1892 and subsequently by Wilde and his immediate entourage. Wilde was hugely amused since the flower meant 'nothing whatever but that is what nobody will guess'. In fact, it represented 'the aesthete's flower', being a symbolic triumph of Art over Nature. It rapidly became one of the more obvious badges of perceived decadence and was still a valid point of reference when Noël Coward wrote a song of that name in the 1929 *Bitter Sweet*, sung by a quartet of effete young men:

> *Haughty boys, naughty boys, dear, dear, dear!*
> *Swooning with affectation...*
> *Art is our inspiration,*
> *And as we are the reason for the 'Nineties'*
> *being gay*
> *We all wear a green carnation.*

Wilde was equally emphatic about the role of the Artist:

Artists, like Gods, must never leave their pedestals.

(In conversation)

The artist is the creator of beautiful things. To reveal art and conceal the artist is art's aim.

To give an accurate description of what has never occurred is not merely the proper occupation of the historian, but the inalienable

privilege of any man of parts and culture.
('The Critic As Artist')

✒

The moral life of man forms part of the subject-matter of the artist, but the morality of art consists in the perfect use of an imperfect medium.

✒

No artist desires to prove anything.

✒

No artist has ethical sympathies.

✒

No artist is ever morbid. The artist can express everything.

✒

Thought and language are to the artist instruments of an art.

✒

Vice and virtue are to the artist material for an art.

✒

From the point of view of form, the type of all the arts is the art of the musician. From the point of view of feeling, the actor's craft is the type.

✒

We can forgive a man for making a useful thing as long as he does not admire it. The only excuse for making a useless thing is that one admires it intensely.

(Preface to *The Picture of Dorian Gray*)

A work of art is the unique result of a unique temperament. Its beauty comes from the fact that the author is what he is… If he does not do it solely for his own pleasure, he is no artist at all.

('The Soul of Man Under Socialism')

An artist's heart is his head, and besides, our business is to realise the world as we see it, not to reform it as we know it.

(Alan Trevor in 'The Model Millionaire')

A subject that is beautiful in itself gives no suggestion to the artist. It lacks imperfection.

('A Few Maxims for the Instruction of the Over-Educated')

But in the next breath Wilde can mercifully bring himself down to earth:

The subject of a work of art has, of course, nothing to do with its beauty… but there is always something depressing about the coloured lithograph of a leg of mutton.

('Dinners and Dishes')

One artist Wilde particularly admired was the American expatriate, James McNeill Whistler (1834–1903), and for some years the two were great personal friends. In Wilde's view Whistler was 'the first painter in England, only it will take England 300 years to find out'.

The painter was something of a wit in his own right and it was in the contest for celebrity that the rift occurred. Whistler was one of the most vociferous over what he considered Wilde's 'borrowing' of the ideas of others – most particularly his. ('What has Oscar in common with Art? Except that he dines at our tables and picks from our platters the plums for the pudding he peddles in the provinces... He has the courage of the opinions of others.')

Later he wrote to *Truth* magazine to complain about Wilde's 'plagiarism' pointing out that in America the offence would cause him to be 'criminally prosecuted, incarcerated, and made to pick oakum, as he has hitherto picked brains'. To begin with Wilde took it as friendly badinage.

In an exchange of telegrams Wilde happened to remark that, 'When you and I are together we never talk about anything but ourselves.' 'No, no, Oscar, you forget,' Whistler replied, 'When you and I are together, we never talk about anything but me.' 'It is true, Jimmy, we were *talking* about you, but I was *thinking* of myself.'

Before long the gloves were off. 'Mr Whistler,' said Wilde, 'always spelt art... with a capital "I"' and later described him as being 'like a wasp and carries a poisoned sting'. None the less, Whistler was 'one of the very greatest masters of painting in my opinion. And may I add that in this opinion Mr Whistler entirely concurs.' 'With our James vulgarity begins at home; and should be allowed to stay there.'

The later years were bitter and when they met by accident for the last time it was in a Paris restaurant during Wilde's exile. No words were exchanged. Later Wilde was to comment: 'My sentence and imprisonment raised Jimmy's opinion of England. Nothing else would have done so.'

🖋

In Wilde's view Art was not some special province of the Artist alone.

> The public should try to make itself artistic.
> ('The Soul of Man Under Socialism')

🖋

> People's appreciation of beauty depends so much on what they see around them... We want to see the homes of the people beautiful, and when that is the case, people will no longer talk of the beautiful at all.

That day, in his view, was far off:

> Modern wallpaper is so bad that a boy brought up under its influence could allege it as a justification for turning to a life of crime.

🖋

> I have never seen a really nice hat rack.
> ('The House Beautiful')

🖋

> On his American tour a woman asked the Professor of Aesthetics for his advice on how to arrange some decorative screens. 'Why arrange them at all?' he enquired. 'Why not let them occur?'

Most writers (or artists) fixate on the Critic as their particular *bête noire* but Wilde professed to see more in the function. In fact, he went as far as to define the Critic as a creative force in his own right. ('Criticism demands infinitely more cultivation than creation does.' – 'The Critic As Artist')

In his own writings it can be argued that he helped turn criticism into art:

> The meaning of any beautiful created thing is at least as much in the soul of him who looks at it as it was in his soul who wrought it.
>
> ('The Critic As Artist')

By the sensitivity of his personal perception of a work of art the Critic could actually create something new and unique of his own:

> The first step in aesthetic criticism is to realise one's own impressions.
>
> ('Pen, Pencil and Poison')

> The aim of the true critic is to try to chronicle his own moods, not to try and correct the masterpieces of others.
>
> (In an interview)

> It is exactly because a man cannot do a thing that he is the proper judge of it.
>
> ('The Critic As Artist')

> The Critic looks in on himself as often as out to the object.

The Critic is he who can translate into another manner or a new material his impression of beautiful things. The highest, as the lowest, form of criticism is a mode of autobiography.

In the Preface to *The Picture of Dorian Gray* – added to soften the initial criticism that the book was immoral and to prove that it was itself a work of art – Wilde added further advice to the would-be Critic:

All art is at once surface and symbol. Those who go beneath the surface do so at their peril. Those who read the symbol do so at their peril.

Those who find ugly meanings in beautiful things are corrupt without being charming. This is a fault. Those who find beautiful meanings in beautiful things are the cultivated. For these there is hope. They are the elect to whom beautiful things mean only Beauty.

Of *The Picture of Dorian Gray*:

My story is an essay on decorative art... it is poisonous, if you like, but you cannot deny that it is also perfect and perfection is what we artists aim at.

It was an explanation that failed to convince many of his personal critics.

None the less, the Critic (with a capital 'C'), important as he is, must not be allowed to o'erleap himself:

> Diversity of opinion about a work of art shows that the work is new, complex and vital... When critics disagree the artist is in accord with himself.

And, of course, there were Good Critics and Bad Critics. Or perhaps there was simply Wilde in contrary moods. He may have forgotten he told his American audiences in 1882 that:

> The first duty of an art critic is to hold his tongue at all times, and upon all subjects.
>
> ('The English Renaissance of Art')

> All critics can be bought; judging by their appearance, they can't be very expensive.

The sole purpose of any form of art in Wilde's view was the creation of beauty for its own sake and he pursued that ideal throughout his life.

The word recurs again and again – always with a capital 'B'. Over the door of the Wildes' Tite Street house he had inscribed the line from Shelley – 'Spirit of Beauty! Tarry still awhile.' The house he named after Keats, his other Romantic idol, that 'priest of Beauty slain before his time', the 'poet-painter of our English land', whose philosophy – 'Beauty is truth, truth beauty' – was the basis of his own. One of his most prized possessions was the original handwritten manuscript of a Keats sonnet, given to him by the poet's niece.

> Beauty has as many meanings as man has moods. Beauty is the symbol of symbols. Beauty reveals everything, because it expresses nothing.

('The Critic As Artist')

> Beauty is a form of Genius – is higher, indeed, than Genius, as it needs no explanation.

(Lord Henry Wotton in *The Picture of Dorian Gray*)

In 1883, Wilde was writing to Robert Sherard:

> In our desire for beauty we are one, and alone in our search for that little city of gold where the flute player never wearies, and the oracle is not silent, that little city which is the house of art, and where with all the music of the spheres, and the laughter of the gods, Art waits for her worshippers.

> Beauty, like Wisdom, loves the lonely worshipper.

('The Young King')

It was always clear to Wilde that he was a lone voice in the artistic wilderness but it never deterred him. As early as 1886 he could write:

> Sometimes I think that the artistic life is a long and lovely suicide, and I am not sorry that it is so.

But even at the end he clung unrepentantly to his youthful conviction that:

> Our Art is of the Moon and plays with shadows, while Greek art is of the Sun and deals directly with things. I feel sure that in elemental forces there is purification, and I want to go back to them and live in their presence.
>
> (*De Profundis*)

He died as he had lived, like Shakespeare, 'a slave of beauty'.

PART TWELVE

NATURE

'Oscar Wilde as Harold Skimpole'
(Bleak House), *1882*

It seems to me that we all look at Nature too much, and live with her too little.

(*De Profundis*)

If Nature had been more comfortable, mankind would never have invented architecture.

(Vivian in 'The Decay of Lying')

IN THE WILDEAN vocabulary the antithesis of Art was...
Nature. And Nature was far from ideal...

> The more we study Art, the less we care for
> Nature. What Art reveals to us is Nature's
> lack of design... As for the infinite variety of
> Nature, that is a complete myth... One touch
> of Nature may make the whole world kin,
> but two touches of Nature will destroy any
> work of Art.
>
> ('The Decay of Lying')

Nature – he liked to claim – persisted in copying Art. What
were London fogs but 'Nature's unfortunate amateurish
attempt to imitate the French Impressionists'?

But, of course, there was Nature – and Mother Nature, a
social rather than an artistic concept.

In his early literary years Wilde embraced the accepted
poetic view:

> Nature lies out of the reach of even the
> greatest masters of song. She cannot be
> described, she can only be worshipped: and
> there is more perfection of beauty, it seems to
> me, in a single white narcissus of the
> meadow than in all the choruses of
> Euripides.
>
> (Letter to Marian Willett, 1878)

But, by 1887, in a letter to Violet Fane he is taking a somewhat different view:

> A capital essay might be written on the

Demoralising Influence of Nature... It is
those who live in the country that Nature
deteriorates.

Wilde now chose to appear as though he considered Nature
in its natural state a poor substitute for the more civilised
pleasures of Town:

Anybody can be good in the country. There
are no temptations there. That is the reason
why people who live out of town are so
absolutely uncivilised.
(Lord Henry Wotton in *The Picture of Dorian Gray*)

It is pure unadulterated country life. They
get up early because they have so much to
do, and go to bed early because they have so
little to think about.
(Lady Narborough in *The Picture of Dorian Gray*)

I feel sure that if I lived in the country for six
months, I should become so unsophisticated
that no one would take the slightest notice of
me.
(Mrs Allonby in *A Woman of No Importance*)

Sometimes he could be whimsical about Nature. Asked if
he was ill:

No, not ill – but very weary. You see, I
picked a primrose in the woods yesterday

and it was so ill that I have been sitting up
with it all night.

(In conversation)

Far from being a haven of peace and quiet, for the habitual
urban dweller the country represented an unlooked for
social obligation. . .

When one is in town one amuses oneself.
When one is in the country, one amuses
other people. It is excessively boring.

(Jack in *The Importance of Being Earnest*)

It could be excessively expensive...

What between the duties expected of one
during one's lifetime, and the duties exacted
from one after one's death, land has ceased
to be either a profit or a pleasure. It gives one
a position, and prevents one from keeping it
up. That's all that can be said about land.

(Lady Bracknell in *The Importance of Being Earnest*)

GWENDOLEN: The country always bores
me to death.

CECILY: Ah! This is what the newspapers
call agricultural depression, is it not?

(*The Importance of Being Earnest*)

From time to time Wilde would 'retreat' to the country to
try and find the peace and quiet he needed to create. He
was only intermittently successful...

Life in a meadow and stream is far more complex than is life in streets and salons.

CECILY: From the top of one of the hills quite close one can see five counties.
GWENDOLEN: Five counties! I don't think I should like that; I hate crowds.

(*The Importance of Being Earnest*)

Nobody of any real culture ever talks about the beauty of a sunset. Sunsets are quite old-fashioned. To admire them is a sign of provincialism... Yesterday evening Mrs Arundel insisted on my going to the window and looking at the glorious sky, as she called it... and what was it? It was simply a very second-rate Turner.

('The Decay of Lying')

At twilight Nature becomes a wonderfully suggestive effect, and is not without loveliness, though perhaps its chief use is to illustrate quotations from the poets.

('The Decay of Lying')

MRS ALLONBY: There is a beautiful moon tonight.

[204]

LORD ILLINGWORTH: Let us go and look
at it. To look at anything inconstant is
charming nowadays.

MRS ALLONBY: You have your looking-glass.

(*A Woman of No Importance*)

✍

I hate views – they are only made for bad
painters. Let us go in – the sound of a cuckoo
makes me sick.

(To Margot Asquith)

Even after his release from prison he maintained the pose
for a while...

I am on bad terms with Nature; I see in her
neither intellect nor passion – the only two
things that make surfaces possible for me.
I allude, of course, to what is termed Landscape.

(Letter to Lester Pollit, December 1898)

But, in the last painful years of wandering, his underlying
sense of beauty – which was by no means an affectation –
gradually took over:

The sea and sky one opal, no horrid drawing-
master's line between them, just one fishing
boat, going slowly, and drawing the wind
after it.

(To Ross)

✍

Today is hot heart of summer; but all the wind is in the trees; the sea is a burning-glass.

(To Ada Leverson)

The mimosa is in flower, such powdered gold-dust dancing in the sun.

(To Turner)

...the high sapphire wall of sea, the gold dust of the sun, the petals and perfumes of southern flowers.

...the sea-birds, whom the wind here blows about like white flowers... the pageant of the seasons; the loveliness of leaf and flower: the nights hung with silver and the dawns dim with gold.

(To Carlos Blacker)

The day is blue and gold, the sun warm like wine, and apricot-coloured: the pine woods change the air to an aromatic: the wind that stirs their branches is pungent with keen colours: and when one walks in green aisles one crushes sweetness out of the fallen needles.

(To H.C. Pollitt)

WAYS WITH WORDS... AND MUSIC

'Quite Too-Too Puffickly Precious!', 1892

The world is a stage but the play is badly cast.

('Lord Arthur Savile's Crime')

Literature has always anticipated life. It does not copy it, but moulds it to its purpose.

('The Decay of Lying')

One should read everything. More than half of modern culture depends on what one shouldn't read.

(Algernon in *The Importance of Being Earnest*)

HARPERS, the American publisher, commissioned Wilde to write 100,000 words on a particular project. Wilde cabled back: 'There are not 100,000 beautiful words in the English language.'

Words! Mere words! How terrible they were! How clear, and vivid and cruel... And yet what a subtle magic there was in them! Was there anything so real as words?

(*The Picture of Dorian Gray*)

There is no literary public in England for anything except newspapers, primers, and encyclopaedias. Of all people in the world the English have the least sense of the beauty of literature.

(Lord Henry Wotton in *The Picture of Dorian Gray*)

Wilde never ceased to despair at what he considered the rabid apathy of the general public towards literature in any form and he chose to believe that this was a failing of his particular generation.

In old days books were written by men of letters and read by the public. Nowadays books are written by the public and read by nobody.

('A Few Maxims for the Instruction of the Over-Educated')

The public is largely influenced by the *look*

of a book... It is the only artistic thing about
the public.

(Letter to his publisher, Leonard Smithers, 1897)

Wilde himself was meticulous in this respect, fussing over
the smallest detail of a book's production and bombarding
his various publishers with his suggestions.

Every possible variant of the written word he found fascinating – and often depressing...

Language... which is the parent not the
child of thought.

(In conversation)

Parody... the muse with her tongue in her
cheek.

(Letter to Walter Hamilton, 1889)

A simile committing suicide is always a
depressing spectacle.

(A criticism in *Pall Mall* Magazine)

His generation greatly admired the polished paradox:

The way of paradox is the way of truth. To
test Reality we must see it on the tight-rope.
When the Verities become acrobats we can
judge them.

(Mr Erskine in *The Picture of Dorian Gray*)

There were writers and there were Writers...

Anybody can make history. Only a great

man can write it... The one duty we owe to
history is to re-write it.

('The Critic As Artist')

History never repeats itself. The historians
repeat each other. There is a wide difference.

Only the great masters of style ever succeed
in being obscure.

('A Few Maxims for the Instruction of the Over-Educated')

But in general:

Writing has done much to harm writers. We
must return to the voice.

('The Critic As Artist')

Most of Wilde's views on literary matters were – if controversial and occasionally deliberately perverse – unexcep-
tionable. But the apparent cynicism of some of his essays,
such as 'The Decay of Lying' and the sexual ambiguities
implicit in *The Portrait of Mr W. H.* (both 1889) caused a
distinct *frisson* in literary circles. This discomfort was
brought to a head with the publication of the first version of
The Picture of Dorian Gray in 1890. So much so that Wilde
was persuaded to add a 'Preface' in an attempt to justify
the book's claim to be a genuine work of 'Art'. He had
already gone on record as saying that:

The fact of a man being a poisoner is
nothing against his prose.

('Pen, Pencil and Poison')

and

> Good people are… artistically uninteresting.
> Bad people are, from the point of view of art,
> fascinating studies.
> (Letter to the Editor of the *St James's Gazette*)

and would go on to assert in 'The Soul of Man Under Socialism' (1891) that:

> To call an artist morbid because he deals
> with morbidity as his subject matter is as
> silly as if one called Shakespeare mad
> because he wrote *King Lear*.

But the aphorism that did much to create the pit into which he would eventually tumble was one that he devised for that exculpatory 'Preface':

> There is no such thing as a moral or an
> immoral book. Books are well written, or
> badly written. That is all.

> The books that the world calls immoral are
> books that show the world's own shame.
> (Lord Henry Wotton in *The Picture of Dorian Gray*)

It was not to be all. In his trials, the quotation was brought up again and again and each time the pit yawned a little deeper.

When one uses the words poetry and prose,

one is merely referring to certain technical
modes of word-music.

(Letter to Will Rothenstein)

Though he scored his greatest successes in other literary
forms, poetry was Wilde's earliest love and probably
remained, in his heart of hearts, his first love...

Poetry... a sacramental thing, and there is
no pain like it.

(Letter to Louis Wilkinson, February 1899)

Rhyme, which can turn man's utterance to
the speech of gods... When a man acts he is a
puppet. When he describes he is a poet...
The world is made by the singer for the
dreamer... No poet sings because he must
sing... a great poet sings because he chooses
to sing.

('The Critic As Artist')

What I love best in the world, Poetry and
Paradox dancing together!

(Letter to H.M., 1885)

Whoever is a poet grows not old; that is
reserved for prose writers only.

(Letter, 1885)

In the persona of one of his many *alter egos* – Lord Henry

[*213*]

Wotton in *The Picture of Dorian Gray* – Wilde spoke perhaps more truly than even he knew:

> Inferior poets are absolutely fascinating.
> The worse their rhymes, the more
> picturesque they look.

> The mere fact of having published a book of
> second-rate sonnets makes a man quite
> irresistible. He lives the poetry he cannot
> write. The others write the poetry they dare
> not realise... Poets... know how useful
> passion is for publication. Nowadays a
> broken heart will run to many editions.
>
> (Lord Henry Wotton in *The Picture of Dorian Gray*)

Poetry and publication have always been uneasy bedfellows at best – as Wilde knew from his early years. As he wrote to an aspiring young author in 1885:

> Believe me that it is impossible to live by
> literature. By journalism a man may make
> an income, but rarely by pure literary
> work... The best work in literature is always
> done by those who are not to depend upon it
> for their daily bread, and the highest form of
> literature, poetry, brings no wealth to the
> singer.

In an 1884 dialogue with his friend, Robert Sherard, however, he took a less depressing view of his 'Art':

[*214*]

WILDE: I was working on the proof of one
of my poems all the morning and took out
a comma.

SHERARD: And in the afternoon?

WILDE: In the afternoon? Well, I put it
back again.

🖉

Wilde was only to write one novel – the 'perfect but poisonous' *Dorian Gray* – but, naturally, this did not prevent him
from having the strongest possible views on the form in
general and on the work of others...

Novels are a bad preparation for facing God
or Nothing.

(Letter to Helena Sickert)

🖉

In every first novel the hero is the author as
Christ or Faust.

(Attributed)

The justification of a character in a novel is
not that other persons are what they are, but
that the author is what he is. Otherwise the
novel is not a work of art.

('The Decay of Lying')

Wilde had a particular aversion to the then fashionable
three-volume novel:

Anybody can write a three-volume novel. It
merely requires a complete ignorance of

both life and literature.

('The Critic As Artist')

One of his characters who did so was Miss Prism, the Governess in *The Importance of Being Earnest*. It is, in fact, her mislaying of her manuscript that causes most of the plot's subsequent complications. She is happy to set her ward, Cicely, straight about the world of literature:

The good ended happily, and the bad unhappily. That is what Fiction means.

By and large, Wilde did not have much encouragement for the modern novel...

The ancient historians gave us delightful fiction in the form of fact; the modern novelist presents us with dull facts under the guise of fiction.

('The Decay of Lying')

... the great and daily increasing school of novelists for whom the sun always rises in the East-End, the only thing that can be said about them is that they find life crude and leave it raw.

('The Decay of Lying')

Few of our modern novelists dare to invent a single thing. It is an open secret that they don't know how to do it.

(Jack in *The Importance of Being Earnest*)

> I quite admit that modern novels have many
> good points. All I insist on is that, as a class,
> they are quite unreadable.

('The Decay of Lying')

There was, fortunately, an alternative. Cecily kept a diary ('simply a young girl's record of her own thoughts and impressions, and consequently meant for publication') and, as she says of it:

> I never travel without my diary. One should
> always have something sensational to read
> in the train.

(*The Importance of Being Earnest*)

Wilde was not particularly generous to his literary contemporaries and – as he saw them – his competitors. Nor, come to that, to his immediate predecessors...

Samuel Pepys (1633–1703) had 'chattered his way into the circle of the immortals... conscious that indiscretion is the better part of valour'. ('The Critic As Artist')

William Makepeace Thackeray (1811–63) 'found no echoes' – nor had Anthony Trollope (1815-82) – Charlotte Brontë (1816–55) was 'too exaggerated' and, as for George Eliot (1819–80), her style was 'far too cumbrous'. So much for Victorian fiction.

He was always aware of Charles Dickens (1812–70). Had he not followed in the man's footsteps as he toured America? And had he not determined that his own achievement had been the greater – even if he was in a minority? The writer, he felt, 'has influenced only journalism'. 'One must have a heart of stone,' he wrote, 'to read the death of Little Nell without laughing.' And when a prison warder in

Reading asked him if Dickens would be considered a great writer today, he could answer – 'Oh, yes, a great writer, indeed; you see, he is no longer alive.'

William Wordsworth (1770–1850) he considered 'found in stones the sermons he had already hidden there. ('The Decay of Lying')

Thomas Carlyle (1795–1881) was nothing more than 'a Rabelesian moralist'.

Alfred, Lord Tennyson (1809–92), 'the Homer of the Isle of Wight', was, frankly, a disappointment. 'He is of priceless value and yet he lives apart from his time.'

He did approve of Robert Browning (1812–89) – with some reservations. 'Taken as a whole the man was great' but 'where one had hoped that Browning was a mystic, they have sought to show that he was simply inarticulate... Meredith is a prose Browning, and so is Browning. He used poetry as a medium for writing in prose. ('The Critic As Artist')

As for poor George Meredith (1828–1909) himself, his 'style is chaos; illuminated by flashes of lightning... ' ('The Decay of Lying')... 'As a writer he has mastered everything except language: as a novelist he can do everything, except tell a story.'

Hall Caine (1853–1931) 'aims at the grandiose, but then writes at the top of his voice. He is so loud that one cannot hear what he says.'

W. E. Henley (1849–1903) 'has fought a good fight and has had to fight every difficulty except popularity'. (*Unpublished memoir quoted by Will Rothenstein*)

George Moore (1852–1933) 'leads his readers to the latrine and locks them in... [he] has conducted his whole education in public... I'm much afraid, in spite of all his efforts, he will die before he reaches the level from which writers start.'

Moore was equally unenamoured of Wilde: 'Oscar

Wilde's talent seems to me to be essentially rootless, something growing in a glass on a little water.'

Thomas Hardy (1840–1928) 'knows nothing of love; passion to him is a childish illness like measles... He has just found out that women have legs underneath their dresses.'

George Bernard Shaw (1856–1950) was: 'a man of real ability but with a bleak mind. Humorous gleams as of wintry sunlight on a bare, harsh landscape'... 'He hasn't an enemy in the world, and none of his friends like him.'

H. G. Wells (1866–1946) was 'a scientific Jules Verne'.

Sir Arthur Wing Pinero (1855–1934) was a genuine rival as a playwright (*The Second Mrs Tanqueray*, 1893; *The Gay Lord Quex*, 1899) – and therefore to be summarily dismissed: 'a stage carpenter and nothing else. His characters are made of dough... he writes like a grocer's assistant.'

Wilde reserved his praise for two contemporaries only...

Robert Louis Stevenson (1850–94) was 'that delightful master of delicate and faithful prose... the transformation of Dr. Jekyll read dangerously like an experiment out of *The Lancet*.'

Rudyard Kipling (1865–1936) 'is a genius who drops his aspirates... from the point of view of life, he is a reporter who knows vulgarity better than anyone has ever known it ... He is our first authority on the second-rate and has seen marvellous things through keyholes.'

As for his sometime friend, Max Beerbohm (1872–1956) – the man who was to caricature him perceptively but, in the end, mercilessly – his only conversational comment on that dapper little man was that 'the Gods have bestowed on Max the gift of perpetual old age'.

Surely, in that strange mimicry of life by the living which is the mode and method of

theatric art, there are sensuous elements of beauty that none of the other arts possess.
(*The Portrait of Mr W. H.*)

I love acting. It is so much more real than life.
(Lord Henry Wotton in *The Picture of Dorian Gray*)

I never write plays for anyone. I write plays to amuse myself. Later, if anyone wants to act in them, I sometimes allow them to do so.

As it turned out, the theatre was to be the public medium in which Wilde's talents could be seen to full advantage. After two turgid (and commercially unsuccessful) melodramas – *Vera, or The Nihilists* (1880) and *The Duchess of Padua* (1883) – he produced a decade later the sequence of four 'drawing-room comedies' on which his published reputation largely rests.

Wilde's was the Theatre of Conversation and it looked like a rich vein he was mining. Two of the plays (*An Ideal Husband* and *The Importance of Being Earnest*) were running simultaneously and successfully in the West End of London when the disaster of the court case struck. Following Wilde's conviction, his name as author was immediately removed from the playbills and shortly afterwards both productions were withdrawn. Neither text was published until after his release and exile, and his forced bankruptcy even lost him his author's rights, though they were restored after his death.

Typically, he was dismissive of what had gone before...

The only link between Literature and the

Drama left to us in England at the present
moment is the bill of the play.

('A Few Maxims for the Instruction of the Over-Educated')

In the modern English melodrama 'the characters have
neither aspirations nor aspirates'. ('The Decay of Lying')

Not that the classical theatre was much better. Having
seen Henry Irving's 1888 *Macbeth* with his beloved Ellen
Terry as Lady Macbeth, Wilde felt constrained to point out
to his friend, Graham Robertson that:

Judging from the banquet, Lady Macbeth
seems an economical housekeeper and
evidently patronises local industries for her
husband's clothes and the servants' liveries,
but she takes care to do all her own shopping
in Byzantium.

He was in no doubt as to what the successful formula
should be, even if he had yet to put it into practice for himself...

All good plays are a combination of the
dream of a poet and that practical knowledge of the actor which gives concentration
to action.

(Letter to Mary Anderson)

...always assuming that you had one or two of the few good
actors to be found...

Just as work is the curse of the drinking
classes, so education is the curse of the

acting classes.

(To Frank Harris)

In interviews he explained how he felt about his own later plays:

> My drama? It's all about style. Between them Hugo and Shakespeare have used up all the subjects: It is impossible to be original, even in sin… the ending is quite tragic – my hero

A playbill advertising An Ideal Husband, *which opened at the Theatre Royal, Haymarket on 3 January 1895*

[*222*]

at his moment of triumph makes an epigram that falls flat, so he's condemned to make false speeches as an Academician.

(Conversation with the French actor, Coquelin)

The essence of good dialogue is interruption.

(Letter to actress Marie Prescott, 1883)

My nervousness ends at the last dress rehearsal... My interest in the play ends there. And I feel curiously envious of the public – they have such wonderfully fresh emotions in store for them... It is the public, not the play, that I desire to make a success ... I am very fond of the public, and, personally, I always patronise the public very much.

At the first night of *Lady Windermere's Fan* (20 February 1892), Wilde made a curtain speech, which amused many but infuriated others by what they saw as its arrogance:

Ladies and Gentlemen, I have enjoyed this evening immensely. The actors have given us a charming rendering of a delightful play, and your appreciation has been most intelligent. I congratulate you on the great success of your performance, which persuades me that you think almost as highly of the play as I do myself.

Of course, he was an over-excited schoolboy showing off, having achieved the popular success that had so far eluded him. But not everyone saw it in that light.

What could not be denied was that Wilde had taken social comedy to a new level. W. H. Auden was to call the plays 'verbal opera'. H. G. Wells wrote that Wilde had 'decorated a humour that is Gilbertian with innumerable spangles of wit that is all his own'.

His second play was *A Woman of No Importance* and, on its opening night (19 April 1893), he congratulated actor-manager, Herbert Beerbohm Tree (1853–1917) by saying: 'I shall always regard you as the best critic of my plays.' 'But I have never criticised your plays,' replied the puzzled Tree. 'That is why,' said Wilde.

General opinion would place *The Importance of Being Earnest*, 'A Trivial Comedy for Serious People', as Wilde's greatest achievement. When it opened on 14 February 1895, he wrote to publisher, Arthur Humphreys: 'I hope you will enjoy my "trivial" play. It is written by a butterfly for butterflies.' Asked by a journalist whether the play would be a success, Wilde replied – 'It already is. The only question is whether the first night audience will be one too.'

He explained the background of the play to Robert Ross:

It is exquisitely trivial, a delicate bubble of fantasy, and it has its philosophy... that we should treat all the trivial things of life very seriously, and all the serious things of life with sincere and studied triviality... realism is only a background; it cannot form an artistic motive for a play that is to be a work of art.

On this particular opening night, a blasé Wilde said:

I don't think I shall take a call tonight... one
feels so much like a German band.

Asked about the body of his work:

They form a perfect cycle, and in their
delicate sphere complete both life and art.

Within weeks it was all over. The curtain had fallen. In
prison he could look back and evaluate what he had
achieved and, therefore, lost. In *De Profundis* he would
write:

I took the drama, the most objective form
known to art, and made it as personal a mode
of expression as the lyric or the sonnet, at the
same time I widened its range and enriched
its characterisation: drama, novel, poem in
rhyme, poem in prose, subtle or fantastic
dialogue, whatever I touched I made beautiful in a new mode of beauty... I treated Art
as the supreme reality, and life as a mere
mode of fiction... penning comedies that
were to beat Congreve for brilliance and
Dumas *fils* for philosophy.

He had finally practised what he preached.

Between me and life there is a mist of words
always. I throw probability out of the
window for the sake of a phrase, and the
chance of an epigram makes me desert truth.

Still I do aim at making a work of art.

(In conversation)

The difference between literature and journalism:

Journalism is unreadable and literature is
unread.

('The Critic As Artist')

However many claims he made for Art in its various forms,
personally Oscar Wilde required an audience. ('I never
write except for publication' – In conversation). Consequently, the easy ubiquity of popular journalism both attracted
and repelled him. It was an itch he could not leave alone.

Edmund Burke (1729–97), another Irish orator, once
referred to journalism as 'the fourth estate' in terms of its
social influence.

At the present moment it really is the *only*
estate. It has eaten up the other three. The
Lords Temporal say nothing, the Lords
Spiritual have nothing to say and the House
of Commons has nothing to say and says it.
We are dominated by journalism.

('The Soul of Man Under Socialism')

If he felt that then, one wonders what he would make of
today's media age. It was a subject to which he would
return again and again...

I am afraid that there is not much to be said
in favour of either the lawyer or the
journalist.

('The Decay of Lying')

As for modern journalism, it is not my business to defend it. It has justified its own existence by the great Darwinian principle of the survival of the vulgarest.

('The Critic As Artist')

To have a style so gorgeous that it conceals the subject is one of the highest achievements of an important and much admired school of Fleet Street leader-writers.

('Pen, Pencil and Poison')

Spies are of no use nowadays. Their profession is over. The newspapers do their work instead.

(Sir Robert Chiltern in *An Ideal Husband*)

Newspapers are written by the prurient for the philistine.

A publicist nowadays is a man who bores the community with the details of the illegalities of his private life.

('Pen, Pencil and Poison')

In the old days men had the rack. Now they have the Press... In centuries before ours the public nailed the ears of journalists to the pump. That was quite hideous. In this century journalists have nailed their own ears to the keyhole... The private lives of men and women should not be told to the public. The public have nothing to do with them at all... The fact is that the public have an insatiable curiosity to know everything, except what is worth knowing... Modern journalists... always apologise to one in private for what they have written against one in public.

('The Soul of Man Under Socialism')

If you survive yellow journalism, you need not be afraid of yellow fever.

(Interview with the *New York Times*)

That was published in 1891. When he came to trial four years later Wilde was to find that what he had written was all too perceptive – except for the final observation.

Even then he could not conceive that England could ever sink to the journalistic depths he had observed during his time in America.

In America the president reigns for four years, and journalism governs for ever and ever. Fortunately [it] has carried its authority to the grossest and most brutal extreme. People are amused by it, or disgusted by it, according to their temperaments. But it is no longer the real force it was.

('The Soul of Man Under Socialism')

In the plays he could afford to be more playful...

> LADY HUNSTANTON: But do you believe
> all that is written in the newspapers?
> LORD ILLINGWORTH: I do. Nowadays it
> is only the unreadable that occurs.
>
> (*A Woman of No Importance*)

✍

> To corroborate a falsehood is a distinctly
> cowardly action. I know it is a thing the
> newspapers do one for the other every day.
> But it is not the act of a gentleman.
>
> (Jack in *The Importance of Being Earnest*)

✍

> VICOMTE DE NANJAC: I read all your
> English newspapers. I find them so
> amusing.
> LORD GORING: Then, my dear Nanjac,
> you must certainly read between the lines.
>
> (*An Ideal Husband*)

✍

> I am quite looking forward to meeting your
> clever husband, Lady Chiltern... they
> actually succeeded in spelling his name right
> in the newspapers. That in itself is fame on
> the Continent.
>
> (Mrs Cheveley in *An Ideal Husband*)

In *The Picture of Dorian Gray* the painter, Basil Hallward,
complains about being 'chattered about in the penny

newspapers, which is the nineteenth century standard of immortality'.

In an interview – with a journalist – Wilde remarked...

If a journalist is run over by a four-wheeler in the Strand, an accident I regret to say I have never witnessed, it suggests nothing to me from a dramatic point of view. Perhaps I am wrong; but the artist must have his limitations.

One of Wilde's last acts in England involved a surrealistic contact with the Press. On his release from Reading prison he was taken by train to Pentonville for the formalities to be completed. On the train he asked the warders for permission to read the *Daily Chronicle*. Permission was refused...

Then I suggested I might be allowed to read it upside down. This they consented to allow, and I read all the way the *Daily Chronicle* upside down, and never enjoyed it so much. It's really the only way to read newspapers.

What a blessing it is that there is one art left to us that is not imitative.
(Lord Henry Wotton in *The Picture of Dorian Gray*)

Music is the art in which form and matter are always one – the art whose subject cannot be separated from the method of its expression; the art which most completely realises for us the artistic idea, and is the condition to which all the other arts are constantly aspiring.

(Miscellanies)

'Oscar Wilde Galop', sheet music

Despite that, music does not appear to have loomed large in Wilde's life. When it occurs in his writing it is almost invariably treated dismissively...

> Musical people are so absurdly unreasonable. They always want one to be perfectly dumb at the very moment when one is longing to be absolutely deaf.
>
> (Mabel Chiltern in *An Ideal Husband*)

The fact of the matter was that people who were listening to music weren't listening to him...

> If one hears bad music, it is one's duty to drown it in conversation.
>
> (Dorian in *The Picture of Dorian Gray*)

> If one plays good music, people don't listen and if one plays bad music, people don't talk... I don't play accurately – any one can play accurately – but I play with wonderful expression. As far as the piano is concerned, sentiment is my forte. I keep science for life.
>
> (Algernon in *The Importance of Being Earnest*)

> Music makes one feel so romantic – at least it always gets on one's nerves – which is the same thing nowadays.
>
> (Lady Hunstanton in *A Woman of No Importance*)

Of course, the whole business was the invention of those

damn foreigners...

> I like Wagner's music better than anybody's.
> It is so loud that one can talk the whole time
> without people hearing what one says.
> (Lord Henry Wotton in *The Picture of Dorian Gray*)

> MABEL CHILTERN: Aren't you coming to
>   the music-room?
> LORD GORING: Not if there is any music
>   going on, Miss Mabel.
> MABEL CHILTERN (*severely*): The music is
>   in German. You would not understand it.
> (*An Ideal Husband*)

> French songs I cannot possibly allow. People
> always seem to think they are improper, and
> either look shocked, which is vulgar, or
> laugh, which is worse.
> (Lady Bracknell in *The Importance of Being Earnest*)

... and what about the *pianists*?

> They are all foreigners, aren't they? Even
> those that are born in England become
> foreigners after a time, don't they? It is
> so clever of them, and such a compliment
> to art.
> (Lady Narborough in *The Picture of Dorian Gray*)

> After playing Chopin, I feel as if I had been

weeping over sins that I had never
committed, and mourning over tragedies
that were not my own.

('The Critic As Artist')

You must play Chopin to me. The man with
whom my wife ran away played Chopin
exquisitely.

(Lord Henry Wotton in *The Picture of Dorian Gray*)

The typewriting machine, when played with
expression, is not more annoying than the
piano when played by a sister or near
relation.

(Letter to Robert Ross, 1 April 1897)

Asked by a fond mother, whose daughter was even then
playing the piano, whether he liked music, Wilde replied,
'No, but I like *that*!'

POLITICS

Oscar Wilde conversing with
the Lord Chamberlain, 1892

A thing is not necessarily true because a man dies for it.

(The Portrait of Mr W. H.)

It is through disobedience that progress has been made, through disobedience and rebellion.

When asked his own political persuasion, Wilde replied: 'an elegant Republicanism'.

WILDE LIVED during the height of British imperialism and gunboat diplomacy. Somewhere in the mighty empire on which the sun never set British soldiers were always at war. Had Wilde been born an Englishman, as the second son he would automatically have been earmarked for the Army.

None of the jingoism appealed to Wilde...

As long as war is regarded as wicked, it will always have its fascination. When it is looked upon as vulgar, it will cease to be popular.

('The Critic As Artist')

On one occasion Wilde and Conan Doyle were discussing what future wars might be like. Wilde's bleak prediction was that:

A chemist on each side will approach the frontier with a bottle.

✍

Patriotism is the virtue of the vicious.

(Attributed)

✍

Discontent is the first step in the progress of a man or a nation.

(Lord Illingworth in *A Woman of No Importance*)

He had little faith in the much-touted political concepts that were supposed to save Mankind:

High hopes were once formed of Democracy; but Democracy means simply the

bludgeoning of the people by the people for
the people.
('The Soul of Man Under Socialism')

Wilde himself began with high hopes of Socialism:

Socialism itself will be of value simply
because it will lead to Individualism [and]
the new Individualism is the new Hellenism.
('The Soul of Man Under Socialism')

But in the same essay he would write:

There is the despot who tyrannises over the
body. There is the despot who tyrannises
over the soul. There is the despot who tyrannises over the soul and body alike. The first
is called the Prince. The second is called the
Pope. The third is called the People.

It was not long before he saw that Socialism – far from
being an ideal fraternity of free individuals – would be
every bit as structured and bureaucratic as any other '-ism',
political or religious. It deserved to be pilloried like the
rest...

The trouble with Socialism is that it takes up
too many evenings.
(Attributed)

MISS PRISM: Cecily... I suppose you know
what Socialism leads to?
CECILY: Oh, yes! That leads to Rational

Dress, Miss Prism. And I suppose that when
a woman is dressed rationally, she is treated
rationally. She certainly deserves to be.

(*The Importance of Being Earnest*)

The British system of government, of course, was always
fair game...

LADY HUNSTANTON: Politics are in a sad
way, everywhere, I am told. They
certainly are in England. Dear Mr
Cardew is ruining the country. I wonder
Mrs Cardew allows him. I am sure, Lord
Illingworth, you don't think that
uneducated people should be allowed to
have votes?

LORD ILLINGWORTH: I think they are the
only people who should.

(*A Woman of No Importance*)

I adore political parties. They are the only
place left to us where people don't talk
politics.

(Lord Goring in *An Ideal Husband*)

Only people who look dull ever get into the
House of Commons, and only people who
are dull ever succeed there.

In England a man who can't talk morality twice a week to a large, popular, immoral audience is quite over as a serious politician. There would be nothing left for him as a profession except Botany or the Church.
(Lord Goring in *An Ideal Husband*)

Picturesqueness cannot survive the House of Commons.
(*An Ideal Husband*)

There is hardly a single person in the House of Commons worth painting; though many of them would be better for a little whitewashing.
(*The Picture of Dorian Gray*)

Really, now that the House of Commons is trying to become useful, it does a great deal of harm.
(Lady Markby in *An Ideal Husband*)

[Lord Fandel was] as bald as a Ministerial statement in the House of Commons.
(*The Picture of Dorian Gray*)

KELVIL: You cannot deny that the House

of Commons has always shown great
sympathy with the suffering of the poor.

LORD ILLINGWORTH: That is its special
vice…

KELVIL: May I ask, Lord Illingworth, if
you regard the House of Lords as a better
institution than the House of Commons?

LORD ILLINGWORTH: A much better
institution, of course. We in the House of
Lords are never in touch with public
opinion. That makes us a civilised body.

(*A Woman of No Importance*)

I assure you my life will be quite ruined
unless they send John at once to the Upper
House. He won't take any interest in politics
then, will he?

(Lady Markby in *An Ideal Husband*)

He thinks like a Tory and talks like a
Radical, and that's so important nowadays.

(Mrs Erlynne in *Lady Windermere's Fan*)

In *The Picture of Dorian Gray*, Sir Thomas Burdon was in
the habit of 'dining with the Tories and thinking with the
Liberals', while it was said of Lord Fermor that, 'In politics
he was a Tory, except when the Tories were in office, during
which period he roundly abused them for being a pack of
Radicals.'

In *The Importance of Being Earnest* Jack Worthing

[*241*]

claims to be a Liberal Unionist:

> LADY BRACKNELL: Oh, they count as
> Tories. They dine with us. Or come in the
> evening, at any rate. You have, of course,
> no sympathy of any kind with the Radical
> Party?
> JACK: Oh, I don't want to put the asses
> against the classes, if that is what you
> mean...?

> You can't make people good by Act of
> Parliament – that is something.
> (In conversation)

But an Act of Parliament – in Wilde's case the 1885
Criminal Law Amendment Act – can punish someone for
being what society considers bad.

During his visits to America Wilde received an immersion
course in local politics which left him ambivalent. On the
one hand he considered that:

> The Americans are the best politically
> educated people in the world.
> ('Impressions of America')

On the other hand:

> Political life in Washington is like political
> life in a suburban vestry.
> ('The American Invasion')

France, as ever, was far more dramatic:

> The error of Louis XIV was that he thought
> human nature would always be the same.
> The result of his error was the French
> Revolution.
>
> ('The Soul of Man Under Socialism')

And as we know, that unfortunate event had much to
answer for:

> To be born... in a handbag... seems to me to
> display a contempt for the ordinary
> decencies of family life that reminds one of
> the worst excesses of the French Revolution.
> And I presume you know what that
> unfortunate movement led to?
>
> (Lady Bracknell in *The Importance of Being Earnest*)

But, as everyone knew, it was the unsung heroes in any
country who kept the wheels of politics turning – in this
case the professional civil servants and diplomats:

> To make a good salad is to be a brilliant
> diplomatist... To know exactly how much
> oil one must put with one's vinegar.
>
> (Prince Paul in *Vera, or The Nihilists*)

> I don't think England should be represented
> abroad by an unmarried man... it might
> lead to complications.
>
> (Lady Caroline in *A Woman of No Importance*)

[*243*]

LADY HUNSTANTON: She was made to be an ambassador's wife.

LADY CAROLINE: She certainly has a wonderful faculty of remembering people's names and forgetting their faces.

(*A Woman of No Importance*)

RELIGION

Oscar working on Salomé, *1892*

Religion… the fashionable substitute for belief.

(Lord Henry Wotton in *The Picture of Dorian Gray*)

Scepticism… the beginning of Faith.

Religions die when they are proved to be true. Science is the record of dead religions.

('Phrases and Philosophies for the Use of the Young')

I don't think I have any [religion]. I am an Irish Protestant.

(To Arthur Balfour)

God and other artists are always a little obscure.

(Letter to Ada Leverson, 1894)

RELIGION WAS A scarlet thread that ran through Wilde's life. The choice of colour was not made on aesthetic grounds but from the fact that he – born into a strict Irish Protestant family – was constantly tormented by the lure of the 'Scarlet Woman' of Roman Catholicism, knowing the family ties might allow a flirtation but never a marriage.

He first felt the attraction during his student days at Oxford. Several of his friends there converted and urged him to do the same. As a distraction he decided to make do with the pomp and ceremony of Masonry and was admitted to the Oxford University chapter in November 1876.

A few months later, though, he is writing to his friend, William Ward:

I now… go to St. Aloysius, talk sentimental religion… and altogether am caught in the fowler's snare, in the wiles of the Scarlet Woman – I may go over in the vac. I have dreams of a visit to Newman [*Cardinal John Henry Newman, 1801–90*], of the holy sacrament in a new Church, and of a quiet and peace afterwards in my soul. I need not say, though, that I shift with every breath of thought and I am weaker and more self-deceiving than ever.

If I *could hope* that the Church would wake in me some earnestness and purity I would go over as a *luxury*, if for no better reasons. But I can hardly hope it would, and to go over to Rome would be to sacrifice and give up my two great gods 'Money and

Ambition'. Still I get so wretched and low
and troubled that in some desperate mood I
will seek the shelter of a Church which
simply enthralls me by its fascination.

By this time Wilde's father had died and the family pres-
sures were somewhat less.

My position is curious. I am not a Catholic:
I am simply a violent Papist... I have given
up bowing to the King. I need say no more.

It was a statement that was to be true for most of the rest of
his life, even though it brought no peace to his soul.

Perhaps the closest he came to autobiography – outside
his private letters – was in what he wrote about Dorian
Gray in 1890:

He never fell into the error of arresting his
intellectual development by any formal
acceptance of a creed or system... no theory
of life seemed to him to be of any importance
compared with life itself... It was rumoured
of him once that he was about to join the
Roman Catholic communion; and certainly
the Roman ritual had always had a great
attraction for him... [It] stirred him as much
by its superb rejection of the evidence of the
senses as by the primitive simplicity of its
elements and the eternal pathos of the
human tragedy that it sought to symbolise.

He amplified the intellectual argument:

> The mode of thought that Cardinal Newman
> represented – if that can be called a mode of
> thought which seeks to solve intellectual
> problems by a denial of the supremacy of the
> intellect. . .
>
> ('The Critic As Artist')

None the less:

> I look on all the different religions as colleges
> in a great university. Roman Catholicism is
> the greatest and most romantic of them.
>
> (In conversation with Stewart Headlam on the day of his
> release, 19 May 1897)

In accordance with his own thesis that serious things must
not be taken unduly seriously, Wilde felt free to coin epigrams about religion, too:

> I sometimes think that God, in creating
> Man, somewhat over-estimated His ability.
>
> (In conversation)

> For what is Truth? In matters of religion, it
> is simply the opinion that has survived.
>
> ('The Critic As Artist')

> Man can believe the impossible, but man
> can never believe the improbable.
>
> ('The Decay of Lying')

The terror of God, which is the secret of religion...
(Lord Henry Wotton in *The Picture of Dorian Gray*)

Religion consoles some [women]. Its mysteries have all the charm of a flirtation, a woman once told me.
(Lord Henry Wotton in *The Picture of Dorian Gray*)

It is sad. One half of the world does not believe in God, and the other half does not believe in me.
(In conversation)

Prayer must never be answered: If it is, it ceases to be prayer and becomes correspondence.
(In conversation)

Never try to pull down public monuments such as the Albert Memorial or the Church. You are sure to be damaged by the falling masonry.
(In conversation)

Heaven is despotism.
(Prince Paul in *Vera, or The Nihilists*)

When it came to the opposite, he would echo Marlowe's Doctor Faustus: 'Why this is Hell. Nor am I out of it.'

We are each our own devil, and we make
This world our hell.
(*The Duchess of Padua*)

⚜

Simple, loyal people; give them a new saint; it costs nothing.
(The Czar in *Vera, or The Nihilists*)

⚜

There is nothing in the whole world so unbecoming to a woman as a Nonconformist conscience.
(Mr Cecil Graham in *Lady Windermere's Fan*)

⚜

The things one feels absolutely certain about are never true. That is the fatality of Faith, and the lesson of Romance.
(Lord Henry Wotton in *The Picture of Dorian Gray*)

⚜

A Bishop keeps on saying at the age of eighty what he was told to say when he was a boy of eighteen, and as a natural consequence, he always looks absolutely delightful.
(Lord Henry Wotton in *The Picture of Dorian Gray*)

⚜

Missionaries, my dear! Don't you realise
that missionaries are the divinely provided
food for destitute and underfed cannibals.

(In conversation)

That new Puritanism, which is but the
whine of the hypocrite.

To be either a Puritan, a prig or a preacher is
a bad thing. To be all three at once reminds
me of the worst excesses of the French
Revolution.

(That excessive French Revolution again!)

No man dies for what he knows to be true.
Men die for what they want to be true, for
what some terror in their hearts tells them is
not true... To die for one's theological beliefs
is the worst use a man can make of his life.

(*The Portrait of Mr W. H.*)

In *An Ideal Husband*, Sir Robert Chiltern suggests to Mrs
Cheveley that Optimism and Pessimism 'seem to be the
only two fashionable religions left to us nowadays'. Which
does she follow? 'Oh, I'm neither. Optimism begins in a
broad grin and Pessimism ends with blue spectacles.
Besides, they are both of them merely poses.'

The reason that we all like to think so well of
others is that we are all afraid for ourselves.

[*252*]

The basis of optimism is sheer terror.

(The Picture of Dorian Gray)

Sin was a topic he frequently returned to – often as 'a form of art'…

What is termed sin is an essential element of progress… By its curiosity Sin increases the experience of the race.

(Ernest in 'The Critic As Artist')

Religion consoles some. Its mysteries have all the charm of a flirtation… Besides, nothing makes one so vain as being told one is a sinner. . . It is in the brain, and the brain only, that the great sins of the world take place.

(Lord Henry Wotton in *The Picture of Dorian Gray*)

If your sins find you out, why worry! It is when they find you in that trouble begins.

(In conversation)

The only difference between the saint and the sinner is that every saint has a past, and every sinner has a future.

(Lord Illingworth in *A Woman of No Importance*)

Sin is a thing that writes itself across a man's

face. It cannot be concealed.

(Lord Henry Wotton in *The Picture of Dorian Gray*)

⟡

Prison gave Wilde both cause and time to think but his own personal dilemma of faith went unresolved. In *De Profundis*:

> Religion does not help me. The faith that others give in what is unseen, I give to what one can touch and look at... When I think about Religion at all, I feel as if I would like to fund an order for those who cannot believe... Everything to be true must become a religion, and agnosticism should have its ritual no less than faith... the Confraternity of the Faithless who *cannot* believe.

⟡

Where there is sorrow, there is holy ground.

However, one thing at least did come into focus for Wilde during those two solitary years. Today we would be tempted to tag it 'born-again Christianity'. He was at last able to see Christ's place in the scheme of things. For all of his adult life Wilde had been preaching the 'religion' of Individualism. At one point he had thought Socialism might provide the answer but it had not. Now...

> Christ, the supreme Individualist, uniting personality and perfection, saying beautiful

things, making of his life the most wonderful
of poems by creating himself out of his own
imagination.

Christ... the true precursor of the romantic
movement in life... Christ's place indeed is
with the poets. His whole conception of
Humanity springs right out of the
imagination and can only be realised by it...

And when Wilde writes of 'the little supper with his com-
panions, one of whom had already sold him for a price',
was he remembering, one wonders, the endless 'little sup-
pers' he and Bosie had sat over at the Café Royal and
Willis's – and their outcome?

After his release, Wilde's first instinctive thought was to
apply to the Jesuits in Farm Street to accept him for a six-
month retreat...

It must be delightful to see God through
stained glass windows... I may even go to a
monastery myself.

(Letter to Belgian writer, Maurice Maeterlinck)

His request was immediately refused. At least a year's
deliberation would be involved. Wilde broke down in tears
and the decision to leave England that very day was confirmed. He never set foot in England again.

In the little French village of Berneval outside Dieppe,

where he lived alone in those first few months, he was in the
habit of going to Mass and Vespers in the local church...

I am seated in the Choir! I suppose sinners
should have the high places near Christ's
altar? I know at any rate that Christ would
not turn me out.

To me, suffering seems now a sacramental
thing, that makes those whom it touches
holy.
(Letter to Carlos Blacker)

More and more he dwelt on the Great Alternative to Life...

Death is not a God. He is merely a servant of
the gods.
('*La Sainte Courtisane*')

Death is the inheritance of us all... Life were
incomplete without it.
(Canon Chasuble in *The Importance of Being Earnest*)

One should live as if there were no death.
One should die as if one had never lived.

I have no terror of Death. It is the coming of
Death that terrifies me. Its monstrous wings

[*256*]

seem to wheel in the leaden air around me.

(Dorian in *The Picture of Dorian Gray*)

He had felt the impact of death early. When his beloved younger sister, Isola, had died in 1867 at the age of nine, Wilde had written a poem called 'Requiescat':

> *Tread lightly, she is near*
> *Under the snow,*
> *Speak gently, she can hear*
> *The daisies grow.*
> *All her bright golden hair*
> *Tarnished with rust,*
> *She that was young and fair*
> *Fallen to dust.*

In 1894 he would write to Douglas:

Death and love seem to walk on either hand as I go through life: they are the only things I think of, their wings shadow me.

In the three years of exile Wilde's thoughts turned increasingly inward. In an interview with the *Daily Chronicle* (the newspaper he had read upside down on his way from prison) just three weeks before his death, he speculated, somewhat simplistically:

Much of my moral obliquity is due to the fact that my father would not allow me to become a Catholic. The artistic side of the Church and the fragrance of its teaching would have cured my degeneracies.

Catholicism is the only religion to die in.

And so it proved. By November 1900 Wilde was confined to his room at the shabby Hotel d'Alsace in Paris. On the 30th, seeing that death was near, Robert Ross, who was at the bedside, took it upon himself to go out and fetch a priest.

Oscar Fingal O'Flahertie Wills Wilde – despite his life-long unorthodox views – was finally received into the Roman Catholic faith and embraced the Scarlet Woman on the day he died.

The Law
and Prison

'The Arrest of Oscar Wilde', 1895

If a man knows the law there is nothing
illegal he cannot do when he likes: that is
why folk become lawyers.

(Peter in Vera, or The Nihilists)

The cruelty of a prison sentence starts when
you come out.

(*De Profundis*)

FOR MOST OF HIS SHORT LIFE Wilde viewed the law with the same wry disdain he felt for most British institutions – it was undoubtedly an ass.

> The criminal classes are so close to us that even the policeman can see them. They are so far away from us that only the poet can understand them.
>
> ('A Few Maxims for the Instruction of the Over-Educated')

> All crime is vulgar, just as all vulgarity is crime... Crime belongs exclusively to the lower orders... I should fancy that crime was to them what art is to us, simply a method of procuring extraordinary sensations.
>
> (Lord Henry Wotton in *The Picture of Dorian Gray*)

> Crime in England is rarely the result of sin. It is nearly always the result of starvation.
>
> ('Pen, Pencil and Poison')

In 1895, during his three trials Wilde was to see the law from a very different perspective.

At the first trial, Wilde was suing Bosie's father, the Marquis of Queensberry, for libel. The choleric Queensberry was best known for two things – his penchant for litigation and for codifying the rules of boxing. When 'the Scarlet Marquis', as Wilde dubbed him – presumable forgetting that the same colourful adjective was one he applied to Rome – came to threaten him in person, Wilde replied, 'I do not know what the Queensberry Rules are, but the Oscar Wilde rule is to shoot on sight.'

In this – as in the two subsequent trials, when *he* was the defendant – Wilde was brilliant as long as he was on safe artistic ground. And until he began to realise just how much damning evidence the other side had accumulated, he could use his wit to deflect or dilute some of the hostile questioning.

Asked about the visit from Allen the blackmailer, who had acquired a compromising letter to Bosie and claimed to have been offered £60 for it, Wilde suggested, 'If you take my advice, you will go to that man and sell my letter to him for £60. I myself have never received so large a sum for any prose work of that length.' In any case, he assured Allen, the letter was, in reality, a 'prose poem', but then, 'art is rarely intelligible to the criminal classes'.

Edward Carson, QC, picked up a phrase from *The Picture of Dorian Gray* – 'I quite admit that I adored you madly.' And went on to ask Wilde:

CARSON: Have you ever adored a young man madly?

WILDE: No, not madly. I prefer love – that is a higher form... I have never given adoration to anybody except myself.

Later Carson questioned him about a 'rent' boy who sold newspapers on the pier at Worthing. Was Wilde aware of the young man's occupation? 'No, it is the first I have heard of his connection with literature.'

In a more serious moment, Wilde was prompted by Carson's questioning to provide the perfect definition of his brand of hedonism:

I think that the realisation of oneself is the
prime aim of life, and to realise oneself
through pleasure is finer than to do so
through pain. I am on that point entirely on
the side of the ancients – the Greeks.

Reading the transcripts tends to confirm the feeling that
Wilde was both actor and spectator, as far as his own life
was concerned. Listening to the prosecution summing up
its damning case against him in the third trial, it suddenly
occurred to him – 'How splendid it would be, if I was saying all this about myself!'

In his palmier days Wilde could say to Carson:

Judges, like the criminal classes, have their
lighter moments.
('Critic in Pall Mall')

If they do, he was not to witness one of them. At the end of
Wilde's third trial, Mr Justice Wills sentenced him to two
years hard labour. 'And I? May I say nothing, my lord?'
was all he could manage before the Judge waved to the
warders to remove the prisoner. They were the last words
Oscar Wilde would ever speak in public in his adopted
country.

Before the doors closed behind him, it was perfectly possible to consider the idea of prison philosophically. In 'The
Soul Of Man Under Socialism (1891)...

A community is infinitely more brutalised
by the habitual employment of punishment
than it is by the occasional occurrence of
crime.

... and in one of his more prophetic assertions...

> After all, even in prison a man can be quite
> free. His soul can be free. His personality
> can be untroubled. He can be at peace.

In 1894 he told an interviewer:

> Never attempt to reform a man. Men never
> repent. To punish a man for wrong-doing,
> with a view to his reformation is the most
> lamentable mistake it is possible to commit.
> If he has any soul at all, such a procedure is
> calculated to make him ten times worse than
> before. It is a sign of a noble nature to refuse
> to be broken by force.
> (Letter to Almy)

But that was *then*... His feelings were soon to change:

> I have the horror of death with the still
> greater horror of living.
> (Letter to Robert Ross, 10 March 1896)

We know of Wilde's mental state in the various prisons –
Pentonville, Wandsworth and Reading – partly from the
occasional letters he was allowed to write but mostly from
the 80-page 'letter' he pieced together a page a day towards
the end of his sentence. Robert Ross, to whom the manuscript was eventually entrusted, gave it the title *De
Profundis*.

It is a remarkable document in the way it charts Wilde's
emotional ebbs and flows over the weeks it took him to
compose it. Each day he would hand over to the warder the

single page of paper he had been given. Next day he would start afresh, trying to keep in his mind what had gone before. It is by turns a subjective exposition of what he felt had occurred, an excoriation of Bosie, a wallow in self-pity and a series of philosophical speculations. It seems to have been printed, once the full version was made available, precisely as Wilde first wrote it and handed it to Ross as he left prison.

For the first few weeks he seemed to be trying – if only for the benefit of his friends – to be true to his earlier belief that the experience need not touch him. He wrote to the Leversons that 'a slim thing, goldhaired like an angel, stands always at my side'. 'My sweet rose, my delicate flower, my lily of lilies,' he wrote to Bosie.

But the mindless weeks and months took their toll and by the time he came to write *De Profundis* he was feeling a lot less forgiving.

After my terrible sentence, when the prison-dress was on me, and the prison-house door closed, I sat amidst the ruins of my wonderful life, crushed by anguish, bewildered with terror, dazed through pain. But I would not hate you. Every day I said to myself, 'I must keep love in my heart today, else how shall I live through the day?' It did not occur to me then that you could have the supreme vice, shallowness...

The gods are strange... It is not of our vices only they make instruments to scourge us. They bring us to ruin through what in us is

good, gentle, humane and loving. But for my
pity and affection for you and yours, I would
not now be weeping in this terrible place.

'Oscar Wilde in Prison', 1895

We who live in prison, and in whose lives there is no event but sorrow, have to measure time by throbs of pain, and the record of bitter moments... Suffering... is the means by which we exist, because it is the only means by which we become conscious of existing.

Prison life makes one see people and things as they really are... The most terrible thing about it is not that it breaks one's heart – hearts are meant to be broken – but that it turns one to stone.

(Letter to Robert Ross)

I drank the sweet, I drank the bitter, and I found the bitterness in the sweetness and the sweetness in the bitterness. The cruelty of a prison sentence starts when you come out.

On leaving prison...

I go out with an adder in my heart, and an asp in my tongue, and every night I sow thorns in the garden of my soul.

(Letter to Reggie Turner, 1897)

I know that on the day of my release I shall
be merely passing from one prison into
another, and there are times when the whole
world seems to me no larger than my cell and
as full of terror for me. Still I believe that at
the beginning God made a world for each
separate man, and in that world, which is
within us, one should seek to live.

(Letter to Robert Ross, 1 April 1897)

By the time of his release, Wilde genuinely believed himself
to be free from Bosie's influence and able to make some sort
of fresh start, both personally and artistically. Writing *De
Profundis*, he felt, had effectively purged him of the malign
influences that had brought about his downfall.

What concerned him most was to capture in words the
experience of prison. In the months in France immediately
following his release he wrote the epic poem, 'The Ballad of
Reading Gaol' – 'written from personal experience, a sort
of denial of my own philosophy of art in many ways'.

In America he had declared that 'The secret of Life is art'
but now he knew better. 'The secret of Life is suffering.'

Although he did not know it, 'The Ballad of Reading
Gaol' was to be Wilde's last literary work. In it he returned
to the muse he had always admired the most – the muse of
poetry – but, in doing so, he set aside the florid versifying of
earlier years and spoke directly from the heart about something he had experienced rather than imagined:

And never a human voice comes near
To speak a human word:
And the eye that watches through the door
Is pitiless and hard:

And by all forgot, we rot and rot,
With body and soul marred...

The vilest deeds like poison weeds,
Bloom well in prison air;
It is only what is good in Man
That wastes and withers there:
Pale anguish keeps the heavy gate,
And the warder is Despair...

Yet each man kills the thing he loves,
By each let this be heard,
Some do it with a bitter look,
Some with a flattering word.
The coward does it with a kiss,
The brave man with a sword.

When it was finished, Wilde wrote to Ross:

The poem suffers under the difficulties of a divided aim in style, some is realistic, some is romantic: some poetry, some propaganda. I feel it keenly, but as a whole I think the production interesting.

Not surprisingly, the subject of prison dominated his letters to his friends for months to come.

The horror of prison life is the contrast between the grotesqueness of one's aspect and the tragedy in one's soul.
(Letter to Leonard Smithers)

I wish we could talk over the many prisons
of life – prisons of stone, prisons of passion,
prisons of intellect, prisons of morality and
the rest – all limitations, external or internal,
all prisons really.

(Letter to Cunningham Graham, who had himself been in
prison)

One of the few friends he made in prison was the warder,
Thomas Martin. In a letter to him, Wilde recalls the experience of attending the prison chapel:

I longed to rise in my place and cry out, and
tell the poor disinherited wretches around
me that... they are society's victims, and
that society has nothing to offer them but
starvation in the streets, or starvation and
cruelty in prison.

By the end of his life he could see little humour in the
British way of crime and punishment:

The present prison system seems almost to
have for its aim the wrecking and
destruction of the mental faculties.

The question was – what had it done to his?

WILDE ON WILDE

'Society's Hopes and Fears', 1882

Each of us has Heaven and Hell in him.
(Dorian in *The Picture of Dorian Gray*)

✤

One can live for years sometimes without living at all, and then life comes crowding into one single hour.
(The Czar in *Vera: or The Nihilists*)

✤

There are moments when one has to choose between living one's life, fully, entirely, completely – or dragging out some false, shallow degrading existence that the world in its hypocrisy demands.
(Lord Darlington in *Lady Windermere's Fan*)

✤

My cradle was rocked by the Fates. Only in the mire can I know peace.
(Letter to Carlos Blacker, France, 1897)

✤

Yet who beneath this night of wars and
*   fears,*
From tranquil tower can watch the
*   coming years;*
Who can foretell what joys the day shall
*   bring...*
(*Ravenna*, Wilde's Newgate Prize Poem, 1878)

✤

Harry spends his days saying what is
incredible, and his evenings in doing what is
improbable. Just the sort of life I would like
to lead.

(Dorian about Lord Henry in *The Picture of Dorian Gray*)

So MUCH OF what Wilde wrote now seems disturbingly
predictive of his own life. Equally, there was an inevitabili-
ty about his actions – and his lack of reactions – that led to
the playing out of the drama he always insisted his life
would be. Even though he could not bring himself to
believe it would end the way it did, in his Celtic soul it was
all *meant*.

At every single moment of one's life one is
what one is going to be no less than what one
has been.

(*De Profundis*)

Wilde went his own way and left the world to follow…

Like Emerson, I write over the door of my
library the word 'Whim'.

(Vivian in 'The Decay of Lying')

Judged by the way that world judges, he was both idle and
arrogant…

I must frankly confess that, by nature and
by choice, I am extremely indolent.
Cultivated idleness seems to me to be the
proper occupation for man.

(Letter to the Editor of the *Scots Observer*, 1890)

[*273*]

The only thing that sustains one through life is the consciousness of the immense inferiority of everybody else… I am always thinking of myself, and I expect everybody else to do the same. That is what is called sympathy… I hate people who talk about themselves… when one wants to talk about oneself. It is what I call selfishness.

('The Remarkable Rocket')

There is only one thing in the world worse than being talked about, and that is not being talked about.

(Lord Henry Wotton in *The Picture of Dorian Gray*)

I am the only person in the world I should like to know thoroughly.

(Mr Dumby in *Lady Windermere's Fan*)

Other people are quite dreadful. The only possible society is oneself.

(Lord Goring in *An Ideal Husband*)

As the supreme Individualist – until he recognised the prior claim of Christ – Wilde was quite clear about his relationship to his society or, indeed, his century…

He who would be free… must not conform.

('The Soul of Man Under Socialism')

I consider that for any man of culture to
accept the standard of his age is a form of the
grossest immorality... To be popular one
must be a mediocrity.

(Lord Henry Wotton in *The Picture of Dorian Gray*)

Lord Henry's friend, Basil Hallward, took a contradictory
point of view:

There is a fatality about all physical and
intellectual distinction... It is better not to
be different from one's fellows.

By the time he came to write *De Profundis*, Wilde had had
ample time to question many of the values by which he had
lived ('a life so charmingly and so wonderfully improbable
as mine') and to discern the pattern in that life that others
had seen much sooner...

I have grown tired of the articulate
utterances of men and things.

What lies before me is my past.

I have come, not from obscurity into the
momentary notoriety of crime, but from a
sort of fame to a sort of eternity of infamy...
From me the beautiful world of colour and
motion has been taken away... Everything
about my tragedy has been hideous, mean,
repellent, lacking in style. Our very dress [*as*

convicts] makes us grotesques. We are the
zanies of sorrow. We are clowns whose
hearts are broken.

I, once a lord of language, have no words to
express my anguish and my shame... A name
made noble and honoured... in the public
history of my own country in its evolution as
a nation. I had disgraced that name eternally.
I had made it a low byword among low
people... I had... given it to fools that they
might turn it into a synonym for folly.

I surrounded myself with the smaller natures
and the meaner minds. I became the spendthrift of my own genius and to waste an
eternal youth gave me a curious joy... I took
pleasure where it pleased me and passed. I
forgot that every little action of the common
day makes or unmakes character, and that
therefore what one has done in the secret
chamber one has some day to cry aloud on
the housetops.

Everything must come to one out of one's
own nature... The virtues of prudence and
thrift are not in my own nature.

'I am certain that I have had three separate and distinct souls,' he told a correspondent.

> My life, whatever it had seemed to myself and others, had all the while been a real Symphony of Sorrow, passing through its rhythmically-linked movements to its certain resolution.

And he could compare himself to Dorian Gray and 'the note of Doom that like a purple thread runs through the gold cloth'.

> The real fool, such as the gods mock or mar, is he who does not know himself. I was such a one too long.
>
> (*De Profundis*)

Then – still defiantly:

> I don't regret for a single moment having lived for pleasure. I did it to the full, as one should do anything that one does… I lived on honeycomb.

> You would sacrifice anybody, Harry, for the sake of an epigram.
>
> (Said of Lord Henry Wotton in *The Picture of Dorian Gray*)

Words were the currency of Wilde's life and work and most particularly the spoken word.

When he met W. S. Gilbert, the librettist who had lampooned him in *Patience*, the older man attempted to put him down. If he could talk like that, he told the assembly who had been enthralled by Wilde's conversation, 'I'd keep my mouth shut and claim it as a virtue!' 'Ah, but that would be selfish,' Wilde replied. 'I could deny myself the pleasure of talking but not to others the pleasure of listening.'

> It is hard to have a good story interrupted by a fact.
>
> (In conversation)

The question of just why a writer writes has been debated endlessly and unsatisfactorily. Wilde's answer was simplicity itself:

> I write because it gives me the greatest possible artistic pleasure to write.
>
> (Letter to the Editor of the *Scots Observer*, 1890)

The quality of his work, he was to reflect later, required 'the intensification of personality' that only silence and solitude could provide. When writing a sustained piece, he would frequently take himself off to the isolation of a rented hotel room to concentrate. One of the many complications that his relationship with Bosie brought into his life was the younger man's refusal to allow him this vital personal space.

> Praise makes me humble. But when I am abused I know I have touched the stars.
>
> (Letter to Vincent O'Sullivan)

> The public is wonderfully tolerant. It forgives everything except genius.
>
> ('The Critic As Artist')

All the essential elements of future life – as well as all the principal characters – are present in *The Picture of Dorian Gray*. In an 1894 letter to a friend, Ralph Payne, Wilde would admit:

> Basil Hallward is what I think I am; Lord
> Henry is what the world thinks me; Dorian
> is what I would like to be – in other ages,
> perhaps.

(In the first draft, though, Hallward was so obviously Whistler that Wilde had to revise substantially.)

Wilde was in no doubt as to how an extraordinary man should behave towards the ordinary world. In an 1885 letter to Whistler he advised:

> Remain as I do, incomprehensible: to be
> great is to be misunderstood.

Although in a later conversation with O'Sullivan he could admit that:

> There is something vulgar in all success...
> The greatest men fail, or seem to have failed.

When the blow fell, he seemed bemused that this could have actually happened to *him*. His insights applied to *other* people...

> I was a man who stood in symbolic relations
> to the art and culture of my age. I treated Art
> as the supreme reality, and life as a mere
> mode of fiction: I awoke the imagination of
> my century so that it created myth and

legend around me: I summed up all systems
in a phrase, and all existence in an epigram.
(*De Profundis*)

… and then, almost pleadingly…

What is true in a man's life is not what he
does, but the legend which grows up around
him… You must never destroy legends.
(In conversation)

(Years later there was to be an uncanny – and unconscious –
echo of these words when a character in the film, *The Man
Who Shot Liberty Valance* (1962) said, 'When the legend
becomes fact, print the legend.')

A dreamer is one who can only find his way
by moonlight and his punishment is that he
sees the dawn before the rest of the world.
('The Critic As Artist')

*Lo! With a little rod
I did but touch the honey of romance –
And must I lose a soul's inheritance?*
('Hélas!')

Even men of the noblest possible character
are extremely susceptible to the influence of
the physical charms of others.
(Gwendolen in *The Importance of Being Earnest*)

The most significant story in Wilde's life was one that defied all the rules of bad fiction. Its protagonist was Alfred, Lord Douglas, known to his friends as 'Bosie' (a corruption – if that is the word one wants – of his childhood nickname, 'Boysie').

Wilde met Bosie in early 1891, more than a year after the publication of *The Picture of Dorian Gray*. It was a book that mirrored their personal story-to-be and expressed the feelings that Ross had released in him five years earlier.

The painter Basil Hallward tells his friend Lord Henry about the young man he has recently met and whose portrait he is now completing:

> I find him in the curves of certain lines, in the loveliness and subtleties of certain colours... As long as I live the personality of Dorian Gray will haunt me... Something seemed to tell me that I was on the verge of a terrible crisis in my life. I had a strange feeling that Fate had in store for me exquisite joys and exquisite sorrows... I find a strange pleasure in saying things to him that I know I shall be sorry for having said... I feel that I have given away my whole soul to one who treats it as if it were a flower to put in his coat, a bit of decoration to charm his vanity, an ornament for a summer's day.

If only Wilde had been able to maintain Lord Henry's objective cynicism. He tells Dorian:

> Time is jealous of you, and wars against your lilies and your roses.

To begin with, Wilde was totally oblivious to Bosie's obvious failings...

> Your slim gilt soul walks between passion
> and poetry.

... a path he would like to walk himself. Nor did he choose to recognise the scandal that was building until Queensberry, Bosie's father, made his feelings violently known.

'The tower of ivory is assailed by the foul thing,' a panicked Wilde wrote to Ross on 28 February 1895. Three months later the ivory tower was in shards and Wilde in prison.

To begin with he maintained his idealised vision of the 'slim gilt soul' that had placed him there:

> To have had you for a part of my life, the
> only part I now consider beautiful, is enough
> for me.

But as the weeks dragged painfully by, his tone changed radically – both in his letters to his friends and, most markedly, in *De Profundis*:

> I also had my illusions. I thought life was
> going to be a brilliant comedy and that you
> were going to be one of the many graceful
> figures in it. I found it to be a revolting and
> repellent tragedy.

For the first time, he was able to see Bosie as other people saw him...

> You had no motives in life, you had appetites
> merely... your defect was not that you knew

so little about life, but that you knew so much
...Your interests were merely in your meals
and moods... your lack of imagination was
the one really fatal defect of your character
... You wore one out. It was the triumph of
the smaller over the bigger nature... my own
proverbial good nature and Celtic laziness...
A brazen face is a capital thing to show to the
world, but now and then... you have, I suppose, to take the mask off for mere breathing
purposes... I little thought that it was by a
pariah that I was to be made a pariah myself
... It was only in the mire that we met.

Perspective is briefly re-established...

Do you really think that at any period in our
friendship you were worthy of the love I
showed you, or that for a single moment I
thought you were? But love does not traffic
in a marketplace, nor use a huckster's scales.
Its joy... is to feel itself alive.

Bosie's friendship was 'intellectually degrading to me' and
deeply harmful to the 'torn and ravelled web of my imagination... My business as an artist was with Ariel. You set
me to wrestle with Caliban.'

He persists in seeing events as part of some pre-ordained
piece of theatre:

It makes me feel sometimes as if you yourself
had been merely a puppet worked by some

secret and unseen hand to bring terrible
events to a terrible issue.

Then resentment takes over…

He once played dice with his father for my
life and lost.

… and extends to the whole of the Douglas family. They
had, he felt, conspired in some way to bring him down. In
March 1897, shortly before he was due to be released, he
wrote to his friend, More Adey:

A family cannot ruin a man like me, and
look on the whole thing merely as a subject
for sentiment and reminiscence over the
walnuts and the wine. People, as somebody
in one of Ibsen's plays says, don't do these
things.

In fact, it was the last line of *Hedda Gabler* (1890).

He had written his own epitaph in 'The Critic As Artist':

Every great man nowadays has his disciples,
and it is usually Judas who writes the
biography.

Bosie was to write several versions of his own testament,
each of them telling significantly different versions of the
'facts'.

Despite all his fulminations, Wilde was never to be free
of his incubus. He would tell friends – 'I still love him; the
mere fact that he ruined my life makes me love him.' And to
Bosie himself: 'For my own sake I must forgive you.' It was

as though he had now recast the play and was seeing himself in the role of Christ.

In prison he was finally able to confront his own sexual nature honestly:

> It was like feasting with panthers. The danger was half the excitement… They were to me the brightest of gilded snakes. Their poison was part of their perfection.
>
> (*De Profundis*)

But he does not win who plays with Sin
In the secret House of Shame

('The Ballad of Reading Gaol')

Prisoner C.3.3 – his identification number and the pseudonym he used when he later published 'The Ballad of Reading Gaol' – left Reading prison. The following day 'Sebastian Melmoth' took the boat train from England to France and permanent exile. As far as England was concerned, 'Oscar Wilde' was dead and gone.

The choice of name was appropriately ironic. He had invoked the martyr saint in an 1877 ode, 'The Grave of Keats'…

> *The youngest of the martyrs here is lain,*
> *Fair as Sebastian, and as early slain.*

… and Sebastian Melmoth had been the Wandering Jew hero of his great uncle's novel, *Melmoth the Wanderer*.

To avoid public recognition he settled in the small village of Berneval near Dieppe. At first, all seemed well and he seriously entertained the thought of building his own chalet there...

> ... and lord of my own maimed life, I would be able to do beautiful work and speak to the world again on an instrument that has, I think, gained other strings, and become wider in possibility of range and effect.
>
> (Letter to Dalhousie Young, 1897)

To Robert Ross he wrote lightheartedly:

> As for your room, the charge will be nominally 2 frs. 50 a night, but there will be lots of extras such as *bougie, bain* and hot water; all cigarettes smoked in the bedrooms are charged extra; and if anyone does not take the extras, of course, he is charged more.

> The two long years of silence kept my soul in bonds. It will all come back, I feel sure, and then all will be well.
>
> (Letter to Carlos Blacker)

> I have learned now that pity is the greatest and the most beautiful thing in the world, and that is why I cannot bear ill-will towards those who caused my suffering and those who condemned me: no, not to anyone, because without them I should not have known all that.
>
> (Conversation at Berneval)

In this period of relative calm he wrote 'The Ballad of
Reading Gaol' and supervised its publication. With that
out of the way, his mood changed. Instead, the instrument
with its new strings played discordantly. The letters take on
a querulous note and he is writing repetitively to Ross,
Leverson, Smithers and others, two and sometimes three
times a day, asking them for money he believes is owed to
him and issuing detailed instructions for them to carry out
and, presumably, pay for.

He arrived in Berneval in May 1897 with the intention
of settling there. By September:

> I simply cannot stand Berneval. I nearly
> committed suicide there last Thursday – I
> was so bored. The weather is too British for
> anything.
>
> (Letter to Robert Ross)

> I cannot stay in the North of Europe; the
> climate kills me. I don't mind being alone
> when there is sunlight, and a *joie de vivre*
> about me, but my last fortnight has been
> black and dreadful.
>
> (Letter to Carlos Blacker)

In fact, he very much minded his own company. His friends
would make the trip from England, stay briefly, then return
to the world he had known. The solution was obvious.
There was one other exile like himself...

> My going back to Bosie was psychologically
> inevitable... the world forced it on me... I

cannot live without the atmosphere of Love:
I must love and be loved, whatever the price
I pay for it.

(Letter to Robert Ross, September 1897)

Oscar in St Peter's Square, Rome, 1900

I love him and have always loved him. He
ruined my life, and for that very reason I
seem forced to love him more… and I think
that now I shall do lovely work.

(Letter to Reggie Turner)

He was to be proved wrong on both counts. He joined Bosie
in Naples but the old pattern of their joint extravagance
with Wilde's now limited means and emotional blackmail
from Bosie soon resurfaced. Now Wilde was drifting,
accepting charity where he could find it, begging for loans
from Ross, his publisher and others when he couldn't. The
letters make pathetic reading. He ceased to pretend to be
'Sebastian Melmoth ('I have retaken my own name, as my
incognito was absurd,' he wrote to Ernest Dowson)…

I know there is no such thing as changing
one's life; one merely wanders round and
round within the circle of one's own personality… My existence is a scandal. But I do
not think I should be charged with creating
a scandal by continuing to live; though I am
conscious that I do so… It is curious how
vanity helps the successful man, and wrecks
the failure. In old days half of my strength
was my vanity.

(Letters to Robert Ross, 1897)

The weather is entrancing but in my heart
there is no sun.

(Letter to Leonard Smithers, 1897)

[*289*]

By the following year he had come to realise that all his talk of resuming his literary career was empty. 'The Ballad of Reading Gaol' was a necessary catharsis but there was nothing else left...

'I don't think I shall ever write again. Something is killed in me. I feel no desire to write. I am unconscious of power. Of course, my first year in prison destroyed me. It could not have been otherwise,' he wrote to Ross. And to Blacker – '*La joie de vivre* is gone, and that, with will-power, is the basis of art.

Peace is as requisite to the artist as to the saint: my soul is made mean by sordid anxieties. It is a poor ending, but I had been accustomed to purple and gold.

(Letter to H. C. Pollitt, 1898)

To Ross: 'I have moods and moments; and love, or Passion with the mask of love, is my only consolation.' To Harris he added melodramatically: 'The morgue yawns for me. I go and look at my zinc-bed there. After all, I had a wonderful life, which is, I fear, over.'

He and Bosie had now parted again – but less than decisively...

I should never see him again. I don't want to. He fills me with horror.

(Letter to Ross, 1898)

In the beginning of 1899 he occupied himself with the pub-lication (through Smithers) of the texts of the two plays interrupted by his scandal, *An Ideal Husband* and *The Importance of Being Earnest*. 'The Ballad of Reading Gaol' had sold well, helped by an advertisement Smithers ran. ('When I see it I feel like Lipton's tea!' Wilde remarked.)

He now nursed hopes of another source of income but was nervous of the public reaction to seeing his name again ...

> I am not sure that they will welcome me again in airy mood and spirit, mocking at morals, and defiance of social rules.
>
> (To Frank Harris, February 1899)

The British public, it appeared, no longer cared much either way. There were other, more pressing concerns – such as the Boer War – to occupy their minds.

Wilde was now literally starving in the Paris that drew him back like a magnet. He was often, he complained, 'confined to the house with a sharp attack of penury'. 'The wings of vulture creditors' were beating overhead. He had written earlier to Frances Forbes-Robertson that, 'Like dear St. Francis of Assisi I am wedded to poverty, but in my case the marriage is not a success. I hate the bride that has been given to me.' Now the situation was even worse.

> Somehow I don't think I shall survive to see the new century – if another century began and I was still alive, it would really be more than the English could stand.
>
> (In conversation)

Another century did begin and he was still alive. The sad thing was that most of 'the English' probably thought he *was* dead. As he had told Ross four years earlier:

> I know that when plays last too long,

spectators tire. My tragedy has lasted far too
long: its climax is over: its end is mean.

He became ill from a complication to an injury to his ear
sustained in prison. Constant treatment became necessary
and a fee Wilde considered exorbitant was demanded for
an operation…

Ah, well, then, I suppose that I shall have to
die beyond my means.

(To his sister-in-law, Lily)

Towards the end he was confined to his one wretched room
in the Hotel d'Alsace. Typically, what concerned him most
was the distinctly unaesthetic wallpaper…

My wallpaper and I are fighting a duel to the
death… One or the other of us has to go.

(To Claude de Pratz)

If I do live again, I would like it to be as a
flower – no soul but perfectly beautiful.
Perhaps for my sins I shall be a red
geranium.

(Letter to Harry Marteller)

As he was lying on what proved to be his deathbed, Wilde
said to Turner and Ross, who were with him: 'I dreamed I
was supping with the dead.' 'My dear Oscar, you were
probably the life and soul of the party,' Turner replied.
    On the day before he died Wilde said to Ross:

Robbie, when the Last Trumpet sounds, and

you and I are couched in our purple and por-
phry tombs, I shall turn and whisper to you:
'The Last Trumpet!' But, Robbie, I shall
add: 'Robbie, dear boy, pray let us pretend
that we do not hear it…'

Oscar Wilde is now buried in the Cemetry Père-Lachaise in
Paris. Over the grave stands a monument designed by
Jacob Epstein with an inscription that reads:

> *And alien tears will fill for him*
> *Pity's long broken urn*
> *For his mourners will be outcast men*
> *And outcasts always mourn.*
> ('The Ballad of Reading Gaol')

Even this he seemed to have anticipated. In *The Importance of Being Earnest* Jack speaks of his mythical and
supposedly dead brother:

JACK: He seems to have expressed a desire
to be buried in Paris.
CANON CHASUBLE: In Paris! I fear that
hardly points to any very serious state of
mind at the last.

ENVOI

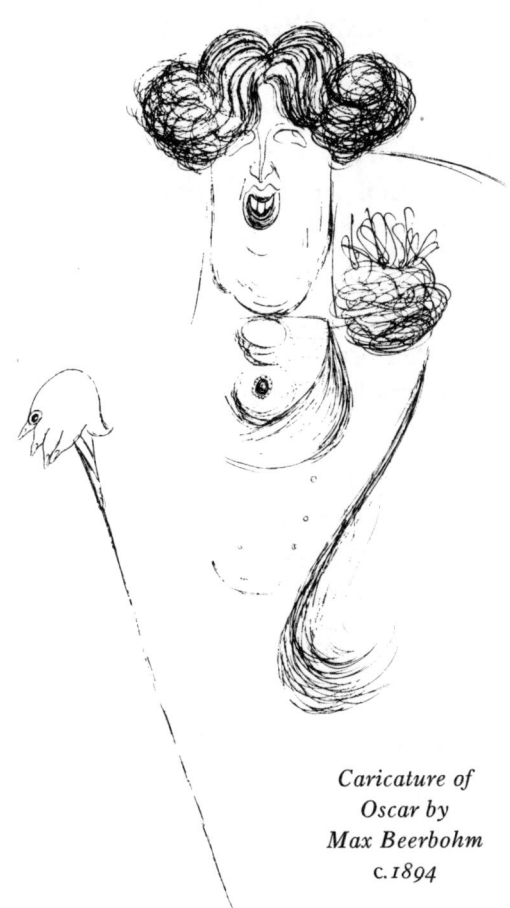

*Caricature of
Oscar by
Max Beerbohm
c.1894*

'We are all in the gutter, but some of us are looking at the stars.

(Lord Darlington in *Lady Windermere's Fan*)

Everyone is born a king, and most people die in exile, like most kings.

(Lord Illingworth in *A Woman of No Importance*)

I shall never make a new friend in my life, though perhaps a few after I die.

(In conversation)

I have never sowed wild oats: I have planted a few orchids.

(Unused line for a play)

If, with the literate, I am
Impelled to try an epigram,
I never seek to take the credit;
We all assume that Oscar said it.

(Dorothy Parker)

THE WORKS OF
OSCAR WILDE

1878 *Ravenna*

1880 *Vera, or The Nihilists*

1881 *Poems*

1883 *The Duchess of Padua*

1885 'The Truth of Masks'

1887 'The Canterville Ghost'
       'The Sphinx Without a Secret'
       'Lord Arthur Savile's Crime'
       'The Model Millionaire'

1888 *The Happy Prince and Other Tales* (containing
       'The Happy Prince', 'The Selfish Giant',
       'The Remarkable Rocket', 'The Devoted Friend',
       and 'The Nightingale and the Rose')
       'The Young King'

1889 'The Decay Of Lying'
       'Pen, Pencil and Poison'
       'The Birthday of the Infanta'
       The Portrait of Mr W. H.

1890 *The Picture of Dorian Gray*
       'The Critic As Artist'

1891 'The Soul of Man Under Socialism'
       The Picture of Dorian Gray (Revised)
       Intentions (a collection including the previously

published 'The Truth of Masks', 'The Critic As Artist', 'The Decay of Lying' and 'Pen, Pencil and Poison')

Lord Arthur Savile's Crime and Other Stories (containing the previously published 'Lord Arthur Savile's Crime', 'The Model Millionaire', 'The Sphinx Without a Secret', and 'The Canterville Ghost')

A House of Pomegranates (containing 'The Fisherman and His Soul' and 'The Star-Child', as well as the previously published 'The Young King' and 'The Birthday of the Infanta')

1892   *Lady Windermere's Fan* (produced 1892)

1893   *A Woman of No Importance* (produced 1893)

Salomé (published in French)

'The House of Judgement'

'The Disciple'

1894   *The Sphinx*

Poems in Prose

'A Few Maxims for the Instruction of the Over-Educated'

1895   *An Ideal Husband* (produced 1895)

The Importance of Being Earnest (produced 1895)

'Phrases and Philosophies for the Use of the Young'

1897   *De Profundis* (written)

'The Ballad of Reading Gaol' (published)

1906   'Impressions of America' (first publication of the lecture)

1908   *Collected Works* (14 vols), edited by Robert Ross,

published by Methuen. As well as all the above
works (with the exception of 'Impressions of
America'), this contained Wilde's reviews,
published essays and the following previously
unpublished pieces: '*La Sainte Courtisane*';
'A Florentine Tragedy'; the poem 'To L.L.';
the full text of 'The Rise of Historical Criticism';
'The English Renaissance'; 'House Decoration',
'Art and the Handicraftsman' and 'Lecture to
Art Students'

1909 *Collected Works,* 2nd edition contained the
previously unpublished poems 'Pan' and
'*Désespoir*'

1962 *Letters of Oscar Wilde,* edited by Rupert Hart-Davis

1985 *More Letters of Oscar Wilde*

2000 *The Complete Letters of Oscar Wilde*, edited by
Merlin Holland and Rupert Hart-Davis, published
by Fourth Estate